I0418493

BOOKS & SMITH
New York Editors

GÓNGORA

ON A

MOTOCONCHO

The Essential Anthology

(1983-2021)

TOMÁS MODESTO GALÁN

A Books&Smith Publication.

Góngora on a Motoconcho

The Essential Anthology (1983-2021)

Copyright © 2025

All rights reserved.

The sale, copy, and/or distribution of this text by any means, whether physical or virtual, present or future, in whole or in part, without prior written authorization from the author or their publishing representative, is prohibited under the statutes of global copyright laws.

This is a work of poetry. References to characters or places with similarities to real counterparts belong to the author's imagination and are purely coincidental. People, events or places alluded to in this work obey solely the protected artistic views of the author and his unique vision—never with an intention of libel or defamation.

English translations by Paige Wilson, Agustín Pedro Klaric, Lucía Ayelen Vallaro, Carolina Bonansea, Juanita Eslava Bejarano, Alyssa King, Pilar González, María Postigo, Carrie Summerford, Lexi Fox, Brienna Fleming, Erin Mangan, Guillermo Contreras, Luke Johnson, and Carley Mills.

Final editing by Edgar Smith.
Front cover image: artepoética Press —permission to use image granted to the author.
Front cover design: Books&Smith

ISBN: 979-8-9889495-5-8

My special gratitude to the outstanding translators (and friends)

who have made this English version possible.

I am forever in your debt:

Paige Wilson
Agustín Pedro Klaric
Lucía Ayelen Vallaro
Carolina Bonansea
Juanita Eslava Bejarano
Alyssa King
Pilar González
María Postigo
Carrie Summerford
Lexi Fox
Brienna Fleming
Erin Mangan
Guillermo Contreras
Luke Johnson
Carley Mills
Edgar Smith

TABLE OF CONTENTS

CULTURAL CROSSROADS
THE GLOOMY GLOW OF BEING NOBODY

ASHES IN THE WIND

A CAVERN JOURNAL

THE IMMIGRANTS' NOTEBOOKS (I)

THE IMMIGRANTS' NOTEBOOKS (II)

SUBWAY LIVING UNDERGROUND AND OTHER CONFESSIONS

THE PERFUME OF BOWLING GREEN

ODDYSSY OF TIME

ECHOES OF THE DIASPORA ARK

POEMS OF THE FIRST DAY

RANDOM POEMS

LOVE ON A BICYCLE AND OTHER POEMS

THE KINGDOM OF THINGS

SONG FOR THE CITY THAT INHABITS US

ALKA SELTZER

DISPOSABLE GOSPEL

SLEEPWALKING CEMETERY

DAKA DAKA DAKA, DREAMERS AND THE TRAIN OF THE DEAD

THE LIMITLESS ISLAND OF LOLLIPOPS

THE WICKED CLOWN POEMS FOR AN ANTI-WAR IMAGINATION

SIGHTSEEING IN THE VALLEY OF THE FALLEN

SHE IS NOT MY TYPE

TROPICAL BARILOCHE

POETIC QUARANTINE SOME POEMS OF 2020

BLACK POEMS A QUEST FOR BLACKNESS

Tomás Modesto, your poem feels like teeth gnashing together—not the grinding itself, but rather the movement that calls for them to the platoon's front line on the hour of the bite: daka-daka-daka, a submachine gun's shot, thirty-two teeth per second to the jugular, thirty-two teeth shot to the conscience. Will it be my turn? Will it be your turn? Will it be up to the corrosive chewing power of Tomás Modesto himself? Suddenly moving from the mouth to the esophagus of poetry, and then to the stomach, intestines and, finally, to the luminous living room of the powerful in the form of shit! Shit for sake of the shit that they make us swallow, Tomás Modesto. Shit for taking surreal account of the state of a corpse, and having to lift New York's cranium from the grave, and now New York is a city of thousands of Dominican corpses who roam the avenues like zombies, forgetting the instructions that nothing happens here, and that the homeland protects the poet's children, friends, non-conforming heroes; and undoes the starved-to-death who elevate the jitanjáforas brought by their African ancestors in their memory of the war drum: daka-daka, your teeth; daka-daka, the poem's teeth; daka-daka, the drum, the fragment and then the click.

I have been assigned the pleasant and complicated task of creating an anthology of the vast work of Dominican poet Tomás Modesto Galán to cover at least 19 collections of poems, some of which remain partially unedited. This has been a poetic and human adventure which began in 1983 and ends (for now) in this year 2019[1], between New York and his half island, the Dominican Republic. Tomás Modesto Galán, Dominican writer of the 70s generation, has resided in New York since 1986. He holds a DEA (Diploma of Advanced Studies —as per its Spanish acronym) accrediting research sufficiency, received upon completion of a PhD project in Hispanic Philology from the National Distant Education University (as per its Spanish acronym: UNED) of Madrid. He completed his master's

---

[1] For this edition, the anthology has been revised and poems from 2020 and 2021 have been included.

degree in higher Education at the Autonomous University of Santo Domingo (UASD—as per its Spanish acronym) and another in Education, Linguistics and Literature at the Center of Education Studies and the Technological Institute of Santo Domingo (CEDE-INTEC—as per its Spanish acronym).

In New York, he works in several areas in the City University of New York (CUNY) and at Pace University; and currently teaches at York College. He was Cultural Coordinator of the US Dominican Commissioner of Culture (2004-2008), where he co-directed the literary workshop Nosotros Contamos and the publications of the cultural bulletin Puente. He is Cultural Coordinator and Commissioner of the Latin American Literary Fair: Open Book, a program of the Bronx Hispanic Festival.

He was a member of the University Cultural Movement (UASD, DR) and the Bronx Council's writing team on the Arts (NY). His first writings were published in the literary supplements of the newspapers: La Noticia, Hoy, and Artes y Letras (DR).

As for the poems selected for this Essential Anthology, or representative of Tomás Modesto Galán's poetry, I must indicate, first of all, that our poet masters many formal registers (free verse, prose poetry, poetic prose, intertextuality, etc.) that are as expressive as the mix of cultures between written poetry and popular Dominican speech. Proof of this is the appearance of English terms, not for an intellectual reason, but because Tomás has been living more than three decades immersed in the English language due to his work circumstances mentioned previously. The poetry of Tomás Modesto is a cultural crossroads, given that memories of his homeland overlap with other memories of his country of residence.

Galán's poetry is eminently urban, a poetry in crisis for times in crisis. Furthermore, it is an insular poetry that starts from a Lorquiano estrangement before the great city of New York. His poetry goes from the deepest lyricism to social criticism in defense of human value, and the crudest sarcasm in the face of said values, not yet in decline, but rather as if they never existed, such as the lofty American dream or characteristic victimhood of the Dominican

Republic, especially with regard to the official cultural life. There are no borders for Tomás Modesto Galán, neither physical nor expressive, not even in terms of literary genres. They are always limitless. He does not even assume the boundaries of clichés, that is to say, social register. For example, his work is riddled with images that better connect with surrealism and German expressionism than with the typical stereotypes of the genre.

In this volume, poems are collected from the books: Ashes in the Wind, Cave Diary, Notebook of Immigrants I and II, The Perfume of Bowling Green, Time Odyssey, The Immobile Ark, First day Poems, Scrambled poems, Love on a Bicycle and Other Poems, The kingdom of Things, Song to the City that Inhabits Us, Alkaseltzer, Disposable Gospel, Cemetery Sleepwalker, Daka Daka Daka, The Infinite Island of Lollipops and The Perverse Clown. All these collections of poems were written mostly in New York—and only some in Santo Domingo.

Antonio Arroyo Silva
Gáldar, Canary Islands, Spain, 2019.

Translated by Paige Wilson

The title of this essential anthology by Tomás Modesto Galán, Góngora on a Motoconcho, fulfills the ages-old task of intrigue and the most modern one of providing information without being obvious. Because a poet of the Culteranismo movement, as was Luis de Góngora, or now Tomás Modesto Galán, travels around the world today in hypertrophied motorcycle taxis (Motoconchos) of the Dominican Republic, the title symbolizes all that appears in this selection of poetry written by the Dominican poet since 1983. In Góngora on a Motoconcho, we witness a constant interaction between the lyrical and the critical, of the literary and the social, if they can be considered different things. The panoptic vision of man, in his labyrinthine existential debate, coexists with attention to everyday detail, with a painful minutia, which attends equally to the most hidden part of the individual and to the most bleeding of the world. In "The Beautiful Nothing," the only poem from The Kingdom of Things included in the anthology, we observe a still life of objects and actions, an exhibit of trifles, which the resonant voice of the poet, rummaging through the cavities of matter, in the depths of consciousness to which the mystery of things throws us, elevates us to the category of metaphysical oil, in the same paradoxical way as Neruda's Elemental Odes. In it, the fertile contemplation of the pots and salt, from lemon and rice, leads us to transcendent conclusions: "I am a name written in the void (...). / I never tire of being a tiger and a man, a woman and a bird. / I am an I, an I-don't-know-what, carrying the you."

In "In no film," belonging to Diario de caverna, we experience a disturbing ontological reflection after a humble session of film: "It happens that when you arrive / you look for the depository of your bones / and you sit naked in the abyss, between a leg that / silences its crying and an eye that curses the night." The Subway Poems Underground life and other confessions, for their part, are claustrophobic compositions, like pieces of soot, but still carnal, and always polyhedral, multifaceted, overflowing with events and feelings, not only narratives, but inquiring into the issues of being, of the substance of man: time, love, loss, death. In them, we find travelers who are urgently needing to rediscover the sweetness of putrefaction, hours lost on the rails of time, errors that roll into the void, trains running towards nothingness, iguana eyes in hopeless tunnels and twilight pubes.

Consistent with this two-faced or dichotomous character, Tomás Modesto Galán mixes registers, chronologies and spaces: in Góngora on a Motoconcho, what is perceived, what is remembered, what is desired and what is aspired to are merged. The poet doesn't mind that Farabundo Martí, Pulgarcito, and the Marines share the poem —as is the case with "To Juan Chacón and the others," from Ashes of the wind— and neither do we. The discourse jumps without pause from one point to another, from the sphere to the rectangle, from discomfort to excitement, from the past to the present and then to the future, but interlocking unalike elements into a common flow, often mighty and always edgy; Thus, they cease to be unalike and become congruent, without losing their strangeness. The verses of Tomás Modesto Galán are not limited to telling: they point, suggest, outline, nuance; and they abound in hybrid and mestizo realities, new realities, whose creatures, always distant and often contradictory, fertilize each other. This is what happens when the poet speaks, in "I need the face of widows," from Cavern Diary, of men who "leave their smile to the noon telephones" or that one "needs to fast in front of a / blue corpse to see a fall in the statistics: the invoked worlds — business, communications, the body, death, the planet— are intertwined to form a new world, a both lacerating and pleasant world, which stands on the page, as Polyphemus stood in the royal octaves of Góngora's, and challenges us from there. The discursive sequence relies on analogical concatenation, the arborescence of the echoes, which are imprinted on the poem —and in our senses— just like reality's stimuli in the retina. The incessant capture of the world by the poet, always observant to what happens inside and outside of himself, supposes an incessant supply of stimuli, which are transformed into words. The result is spermatic, strung-together poetry: a kaleidoscope of sensations. The images follow one other, accumulate, flourish, exuberant, in the verses and spread aroma and color. The poem results in a mixture of delirium and reasoning, in which stands out the fusion of material and immaterial elements. Lyricism, a poem's final glue, saturates and engulfs the poetry.

The critical factor constitutes one of the foundations of Tomás Modesto Galán's work. The denunciation of the tyrant Trujillo and the endless oppression of Spanish-American dictatorships surface in the first book, Ashes of the Wind. "Elegy to Ramón Galán" remembers the brother assassinated by Rafael Leónidas Trujillo. And in "Fictitious Letter of the 2008 USA Dominican commissioner of culture's resignation", he mentions the sinister Johnny Abbes García, head of Trujillo's Military Intelligence Service –who would walk around the Government Palace reading a history of torture, from the ancient Chinese to the contemporary Nazis, both for pleasure and for work: to update their techniques– and the executor, by order of the Generalissimo, of the Mirabal sisters, whom Tomás Modesto Galán also brings to his verses in "Predatory Dictatorships." But the desire for justice that Góngora on a Motoconcho's poems prove is not limited to the American continent, but spreads to the whole world, gripped by a capitalism that sows inequality and suffering. Berta Cáceres, the Honduran environmentalist murdered by hitmen from an energy company; Edward Snowden and Julian Assange, traitors persecuted by the CIA; the clown and criminal Rodrigo Duterte, president of the Philippines; the world's emigrants, expelled from everywhere and drowned in any sea; the tragic situation in Somalia and Palestine; the wars in Syria, Yemen, and Afghanistan; racism, which seems inextricable from humanity; femicides; the harmful nonsense of Donald Trump, and even the shame of Spain's Valley of the Fallen, now happily resolved, along with many other figures and phenomena, draw a strange panorama of sarcasm and pain. It is a kind of medieval pandemonium, reborn in the contemporary world, in which the fools dance with the destitute and the executioners with the victims. Even the Pope displays his zucchetto, but not in a good light, in "The Great March for Our Lives," from The Perverse Clown.

Poems for an Anti-War Imagination: "This Argentine Pope is too progressive / to save civilization / from the piety of Christianity," the poet writes. Civic concern for recent world events can be found throughout the entire anthology and reaches today, in an intense exercise of relevant poetry, with the last poems of the selection dedicated to the global crisis caused by coronavirus.

The poetry of Tomás Modesto Galán possesses a great verbal strength. Urgent and urban, exalted and melancholic, plastic and muscular, it frequently uses vocabulary of the body, which endows it with an imperious materiality. In "Disenchantment with Realism," for example, we find hearts, footsteps, looks, loose hairs, feet, transfusions, caresses, "constant kisses between lungs or common clavicles," hands, feet again, and also, "the body and its ramifications," breasts of "flowers falling behind," furious hands, pulses, another lung, another heart, more hair, nails, the body now "covered with deafening words," hands again, palms of the hands and, finally, heads: a display of organs and pulses that are intertwined with ports, seas, dreams, baseball games, horror movies, and bronze statues. Eros is very present in Góngora on a Motoconcho: "Your lips," from Love on a Bicycle and Other Poems, professes a burning metonymy, and concludes: "I feel your teeth gnawing on an aged bread, / opening to engulf a mangrove, / they absorb the skeleton of an umbrella, / they claim the beginning of this orgy." But the love invoked by Tomás Modesto Galán is not merely physical, being very much so. The figure of a woman emerges in the poems as an archetype of good. Women take care of the world and leave a blessed legacy. The exuberant diction in Góngora on a Motoconcho settles on the free verse to present itself without restrictions. The generally long poem allows a lengthy flow, a branching structure, which feeds itself with the incessant emergence of what is seen, remembered or longed for. The formal plurality, ranging from short verse to long verse and prose poetry, obeys the search for the best expression, the most precise elocutive structure. The adjectivation is bold, like everything in this poetry, but it is the adjective that always gives measure of the author's creative ambition: "petulant horns", "bleeding butters", "monotonous chalks", "happy atrocity", "perfumed genocide", "stormy clitoris". Tomás Modesto Galán is extravagant throughout Góngora on a Motoconcho with powerful images and expressionist touches. In "If Nails Gallop on The Bleeding Back", from Song to the City that Inhabits Us, we see a city that "howls like a bilingual cockroach" and then "throws sewage to scare away winged rats." The creationist vigor, that continues the related traditions of Lautréamont and Whitman, whom he quotes, as well as his brilliant Dominican disciple, Pedro Mir. He sometimes touches upon his work which is filled with the tension of Tomás Modesto Galán's poetry, who does not hesitate to accept the biblical tradition, as he does in the disposable Gospel Poems, and, at the same time, illuminate phonic poems, such as "Daka Daka Daka", from Daka Daka Daka. Dreamers and The Train of the Dead. The paradoxes sizzle in Góngora on a Motoconcho, the outcome of rupture, but also of the desire for harmony, and not only conceptual paradoxes – "torrential sigh", "motionless rain," but also the perceptual one: synesthesia such as "to your deaf pants / the blindness of my fingers". This Admirable vigor, this word that creaks and meditates, reaches even the most recent poems, although, in the last stretch of the work of Tomás Modesto Galán, loses its steam a little, tightens more, and sticks to the bones: to the transparent and polychrome bones of true poetry.

Eduardo Moga

Translated by Paige Wilson

GÓNGORA
ON A
MOTOCONCHO

The Essential Anthology
(1983-2021)

"What is mine
is a man
alone and imprisoned in white
a solitary man who defies the white screams
of the white death
(Toussaint, Toussaint Louverture)
He is a man who fascinates the white hawk
of the white death
a man alone in the barren sea
of the white sand
an old mulatto raised against
the waters of the sky
Death paints a radiant circle
over such a man
Death plants stars slowly above his head..."

Aimé Cesaire
Notebook of a Return to My Native Land

Translated by Paige Wilson

I would like to thank my mother Pascuala de los Santos. She was everything—even the impossible. She departed on April 24th, 2018. I must not forget my father, the large family of my island —my island split into two sad pieces— nor the family from the Bronx that encouraged me to keep going, another black island. Thank you for your patience and support. They paid the highest price.

I am grateful to all my past students, colleagues, poets, and teachers, unaccounted for at all levels, for the share they contributed. To the pillars of decolonizing culture for giving me the necessary strength to carry out this march toward strengthening a better definition of identity.

Thank you to all from my splendid anonymity. I am simply the project of a new man. I still have hopes of representing the best of my generation.

Tomás Modesto Galán

Translated by Paige Wilson

ASHES IN THE WIND

Santo Domingo, DR, 1983

Translated by Paige Wilson.

News

In Washington,
Marx has dined with Reagan
Wall Street sweats a healthy Marxism
In Jacqueline's legs hell is born
the cassock crinkles, unfastens
America has ears sex tenderness children
says its bad words any day
of the *siesta* eating its *guarapo*
It goes to bed with the sirens.

Castaways waiting on the roof

Ambushed by themselves
abandoned in their revelation
their hands had no end
rain produced more darkness, more lips
definitively the weather rebelled
in the cavities of madness
there was no more hair
a strike of lightning undid the lipstick
when the doors closed
the stagnant cry returned a fish,
a dissolved melody
before dying we went out in the rain again
more darkness, we were full of water
there was no one near the roof
in the confines of the wind, a converted vapor
a rain falling upon a castaway.

In cell number one

Sandals without eyes
some books
bleeding nose
beards without cassocks
lullabies
proverbs
solitary spinning tops
chopped trees
ecology of memories
imaginary unions
beginning of paleontology
a quote
the fetuses sing.

A poet's tomorrow

On purpose today is cold
things decompose
it would be incomprehensible to my moths
                                    to my dust
I have the rain waiting for October to close
her consonant growls
with all her thirst for flowers
yellow on the descent of the staircase
I finished writing her memory to the fear
of those who insure life.

Counterpoint to a Salvadoran tale

Once upon a time there was a wolf
that allowed himself to be frightened
by his shadow
—a broom made him sweat
glued to the walls
crazed valleys published their press releases
barefoot goblins participated in the agendas
a family of birds rose green
the grandfather volcano, uncle sun
foams of Coelenterates inverted the minute
seconds bleed, hours are returned
the lake rings its bells
the month is filled with colonels, walls, convicts
the lilacs bundle their backpack
on their spinning wheels
the road takes its toll
flame insects present the credentials of hatred.
Summer passes between plow and heart.
On the lips of the wolf, blood leaves fall.

Parable

Short of days
man
(backbone of existence)
studies geometry
squats in the hands of God
stands among the living
Fed up with light, man blinks without a voice
becomes horizontal over Eve's body.

Child in front of the glass

The child hits the glass
surrenders to the texture
transparent flees from his face
under a shadow frame,
between page and dust, enter dispossessed habits
the rain grazes on the outskirts
copies his tenderness
on the south side of the doors glimpsed steps
of drained air fall with their metallic whisper
the child produces a suffocation by immersion
between the scattered pillows
the last cushion resists
the pliers attack
finally the child spills
in his mother's eye that is already windy.

I mend your hair

In this blurry month
your neck
wild in my mouth
border of lichen
cherry tree drowned between two rivers
writing questions
thinking about food for the birds.

Castaways

Nothing can rust the castaway's teeth
a turn toward absence
a whole sky falls on the gravels
of the sea on the plains of purity
the drowned can no longer be heard
he receives the tide by touching it
as an obligation, he wields the blurred face
of a crowd of drowned men who have
grown slimes of peaceful solitude
paces the darkness
It's a rumor
no one knows who flies at this absolute hour
the castaway is never alone
in the bottom of the hinges
the sea asked many of them for their papers
Some appeared on the shore of the island
only divers, undocumented tourists
and castaways are allowed.

Nicaragua

Between the hoe and the rifle.
Among birds that make Nicaragua
more *Nica* and more *Agua*
between dark deported hands
the pijul sings; the chant of palm trees
is heard elsewhere
and the sky is a blue blur.
From the air comes a scent of *ceibos*
we have already crossed
the flower's beautiful song,
my guitar reaches the swelling general.
What I would give to follow in
your footsteps, Pedrón,
raid a mine, spend the night in Telpaneca!
My general, rest
the pijul has begun to sing
its multiple voices exude auroras
Coyol and Quetzal in the branches
I, behind, general, with my guitar on my shoulder
with the last palm trees under the rumbling cry
                                        of the tigers.

I followed you, general,
on every return to Nicaragua
from Estelí's rubble
to Leon's pain to Masaya.
It is the determined consecration of fear.
There:

     Palenques
     Lagoons
     Bays
     Mines
     Bananas
     Coffee plantations
     Cornfields
          only for Nicaragua!

Down with the gangster, dammit!

His bestial footsteps
were made in New York.
He promised Americans to *somozize*[2]
the national territory
staining the stones with blood
preaching the new code
in a dialect learned in the classroom
FROM WASHINGTON
(IT'S BECAUSE WE STARTED TO BE MEN)
And Sandino is in Chinandega
at the exact moment Managua burns.
Leon is a manna of blood
where the mockingbird flies
above the purest corpses.
The gangster trembles,
urinates and something else...

His eyes let out the gleam of a bat
fear wrinkles his lapel.
Already in the hills the children are free.

The birds are more Sandinista than ever.

---

[2] A verb coined by the poet from the word 'Somoza' —last name of Nicaragua's dictator: Anastasio Somoza.

To Juan Chacón and the others

Hidden in the stairs
I will raise the vigor of my roots
blue won't be worth it
in your marine's handkerchief
the wounding of your little generals
nor all your ships
those wrapped-up lies in banana peels
the pain of your dollars
the dust of the *Farabundos*
collects against you.

The deer has returned.
The orchids bleed.
The merciful prowl the earth
making Tom Thumb sing under the holes;
the strong shadow delaying the afternoon
                              and other dreams
but Tom Thumb went out to sing
at the mouth of the river
the wolf hid in a bonfire
we had burned rose bushes
the solitary cry of children
the vines standing in front of our graves
Tom Thumb sang
the grief of the rocks, the cliffs,
the sad sorrow of the bays,
the death of owls
with the first star.

Elegy to Ramón Galán

(One of the last crimes of Trujillo's tyranny)

My mother and I believed in hope
my brother disappeared one afternoon
it rained over the *quinielas*
my father mixed mortar in the factories
he thought we could survive.

From time to time,
he would see my brother knock
on our doors, dance rock-and-roll
get lost in cars led by the police
                secret and cruel
we looked among the cut branches
for his black complexion
his black mane among the night dancers
the Autumn of his gaze in the newspapers
however, he could come out of a long dream
dancing that old rock of the '60s.

Twenty years, and this habit of ours
of preserving the prettiest parts of you
may seem incredible, the smell of cement,
the serious naivety of those
who don't know suffering
the mornings were for building
the house of gifts
It is true that we had no strength left:
We lost it thinking about the taste of
strange flowers fallen on the foundations
                      of homes.

II

What could we do?
Where could we go desperate to find you?
There is a lot to do and see these days
in which going out to the streets to say bright things weighs down
on my shoulder blades
—like an iron cross.

Sometimes certain habits are lost

My face loses its dreams in the streets,
who would have told me a complement
(of his loss) was necessary to think?

Today that the words come
out of me suddenly
and this tear is hidden

He's twenty years old
Who will strip away closeness?
It torments me to think of your last cry.

We were not there to convince the murderer
of the futility of your death,
a laugh is not destroyed like that,
an indestructible life,
you didn't have to leave your body there,
still fresh, sweaty, finishing your last dance

III

The dust in this photo slips through my fingers
and the only strange thing is that you won't answer my questions,
you who read the newspapers of the fourteenth, you will see how
serious and decent you are.
You don't even show up putting on your new shirt.

Just bought.
Nor will you read the letters
written to your last address.

Amen.

A CAVERN JOURNAL

(New York, 1986-1988)

Translated by Agustín Pedro Klaric.

The body that now bends

The body that now bends
does not concur with the girl lying on the carpet
does not gather her lilies over the light of day.
The foot, free of its root,
hurries an absence of leaves,
a rushed parting of shadows,
maybe the content that faints
between the linen
started over by the closeness
to a forgotten trivial edge.

The body driven to tears and the silent reflection
of her shadow to the linear capital of a back searching for its fall
when the confessions come.
Her naked legs over the spasm of models
end ablaze with two spears turned to ashes
Her bare chest cannot endure the frost
or the widowhood of empty trousers.

This time on Fridays
we all move to the far away chair
or there we rest the thirst of an ankle imprisoned
by the expected eternity in your body,
an abyss restrained by the midday fabrics,
a hope visibly abandoned.
Her hair charms the privacy
of an unexpected summer.

The hand never clenches its fingers
It is the sexual boredom of an eyelid
opened in the instant
when the table eats a second skin.

A flatland ended by the dull desire of arrival.

The chest is born with the description of emptiness.
After the synonymy of breasts,
the bell, the turmoil of a second leg,
the late flourish, the head that happens
to be humid like a dead end
so it goes, the train throws us cans, cigars.
I adore these pots,
your useless gesture when you travel by my side
like a diamond on the skeleton's finger.
But the spite can arise moist by its night,
completely riverlike, like the hand
that unties my legs, the eye that devises
the useless body with its many messages.

I need the face of widows

I need the face of widows entering corridors
silent by the afternoon, limping with foreign pain,
bequeathing their smile on the midday phones.
I long for the pure face of a widow
                weeping for her dog.
I envy it—and I even demand an orchid from it.
The widow weeps
but pain never rises from the handkerchief.
Her pain often steals her breasts, her hair,
her shy retreat. I long for that melancholy
where the pain matures and purifies
I need that hair, those extravagant hands
that everyone stares at before staring at
the corpse, one must not eat before a
blue corpse to spot a drop in the statistics,
a simulation of hair around a still reef
over the dark lines in the room.

Peeling off magnets

Peeling off magnets or playing a game
of magnetizing grapes or the damned
game of fruits that sing in your body
whose magnets recreate a vision of signs
which in time hide the magnet that compresses hands,
and the girl brings flowers, photographs full
of a permanent magnetizing of nails, of lonely hairs,
as if unexpected happiness could move objects until
we forget the age of the doors
or tables that bring memories of bells,
that table reduced to six
when the equilibrium of hands
or the loss of balance ends in crisis
before it rushes us to place letters
on the surface of a cold hand.

Without an eye that magnetizes melancholy
or the widow nails of solitude,
the girl throws magnets to nowhere
and catches black grapes
The green shade adopted by the imprisoned magnets
in her hands or the violet restlessness
Of endless blue discovery or the yellow magnetism
of two bodies that segregate their magnets.
Crossing the room,
the girl takes the magnets to her chest
and there she feels a gravity of free magnets
Sometimes the bodies fall together
and clash with the carpet.

It creates a spark of fruits
on the wall that no chest can hold.

The house tastes

The house tastes its pleasure
writing on the eyes of witnesses,
the shaky pine creaks in the hands of the one
who cuts my sleeves, the one who drives
my legs, my height to the silent fabric,
a pleasure that never mates with trousers.
I am not the one who visits the trivial hell,
you are not the white mouth
at the end of the stairs, the untouched steps
in the restless fever of the paint,
you are not the one who sells your window
for the most indifferent look, screaming
Open your endless body to the infection
of smoke, to the passion of a fire in the spine.

From the filthy attic we have traveled through
an ulna of clarity, shining the stickers,
the snowy radius, the TV made of bras
falls inappropriately on the temple
                    of the sleeping one.
Thinking can be a dark female habit,
an abandoned bottle of urine among medicine.
There are looks (eyes) with no chance of iris,
an unburied observation of things presumably
observed, the reverse hides the nominated geometry,
the pleasing hand of an organ,
the attic stores wind instruments,
the smoke plays its melody,
the mantle, the cry, the spasm
rely on strange instruments;
the strings, disheartenment embitters,
writes a lament when a wind is about to be born
                            on the edge of a hand.

Angry men have run from him,
grand men become human with ink,
with no one's draft,

the cutlery treasures a mouth that is barely kissed,
an almost human pain
If an intruder were to observe it
he would notice flowers among unopened letters.

The everlasting chaos

The third color of the stairs
remains in the everlasting chaos
that starts green and ends blushing
the stranger's descent who does not remember anything
like the stairs—That choose not to remember itself,
like destiny in the steps of an exile.

Outside the wind tears down the shadows
of old companies or drives the last screams of the day.
My eyes will be the echo of that door or of the wind
that anticipates the frenzied bird of my hands.

Very close to a sky made of receivers,
the strangers observe the nearby doors,
the opposite shield, the second to last ledges,
the new birds that a beautiful woman
                        throws to the wind.

The stranger that rules time perfectly
and has defeated rest in the irreversible memory
of some glass can barely notice
the determination to replace the fruits
and cannot see the nearby descent
or the future opening in the envelopes.

The new inhabitants leave before
the caressed words of the mirror.

In no theater

Unfortunately, one is alone in no theater.
Outside you find traces of hair
            and no body lasts.
We assume that, when we leave in a hurry,
we neglect fear, passion, the cigarette,
the keys, the tie.
What happens is when you arrive
you search for the keeper of your bones
and sit naked in the abyss, between a leg that
silences its cry and an eye that curses the night.

THE IMMIGRANTS' NOTEBOOKS (I)

New York, 1992

Translated by Agustín Pedro Klaric.

The disenchantment of realism

Lost love,
unfinished dream of lost pigeons
in the confinement of shadows.
Your return calls a boiling rain,
sweet heart inconceivable in the palm trees.

Steps in the forts,
it would make sense to define spaces
where the eyes conceive clarities,
hollow freshness
that we definitely share.
Oh, things promised to an afterward,
irreversible goodbye.

I sleep convinced by blurry reasons,
dissolved between your undone jet-black hair.

Feeling of lonely seas,
civilizations lost in the twilight oceans
of today or yesterday.
Oh, ancient beaches of sleep,
dot dot dot
preceded by a tiger's infamous steps
in the scorching midday.

Dream, flatland of a mistaken pain,
mutual awakening, littered apologies
in the parks of a first day,
talking over and over until we get tired of our feet.
Transfusion, the exercise of wanting to freely
wish to achieve a walk with no path,

living between delayed caresses,
unceasing kisses among regular lungs
or collarbones, Siamese twins frozen
in a stubborn fall.
Oh, pleasures held by the rain,
undefined road of thorns and roses,
a sea of roses and thorns,
searching for you between the waves
and the sky moistened by the dream.

I have given you my hands, my feet,
and the map that our feet modify
and for no reason I write mistaken confessions
or truths no one can ever scrutinize,
and the speech made of powerless salt,
pepper of the secret utopia of time,
stops chasing sweetness.

Oh, roses of throneless flood,
away from the poem, the body and its branches.
Oh, chest of stagnant flowers
uncovered in the passion of a scent.

Your realism has made me sleep like a god,
unintelligible, what a way of rehearsing answers,
hollowly edited by intellect
that has nothing to do with love.

Talking about escapes, clumsy land, fury,
hands that call your name, the feeling
that hours ago you were beating
on this left side, not even the invisible lung
opens an escape towards the urban hell
that remains on the grass.

Incomprehensible realism, suspicious heart.

Oh, hairs torn by my nails,
prone to oblivion,
a body covered in silent words,
moving roads and expired promises,
trips with no craving for palm trees,
a suspicious and fortunate port,
our letters are thrown to sleepless seas
where we stare at each other unknowingly
until we disappear among the childish
                              songs of longing.
I dream willingly,
a strike that burns our palms,
a ball that cannot be caught in the sinister detours,
a being whose street we slept on
              until we remembered miserable statues;
they overshadow stubborn days and brief springs.

Oh, bridges made of toys
that hang over our heads.

We used to play love from walls
now gone in the marble of wind.
Ours was the noise and an amber smell,
that fear of exchanging looks
in the dull course of a royal ship.

Broadway started from zero centigrade
and that bronze statue where we did not
exchange looks as if a horror movie was shooting
under Fulton's shadow, premonitory stones
that made us travel through
smoke-designed regions.

And that smell of not leaving,
missing a speculation in the window
shot by the rehearsed bustle
of the lurking summer.

Seaport

The river others used to watch,
vain bed of the dead,
born out of the need for a face,
pure melancholy, God's imagination
at that time of full bases,
zero time and a written mistake,
vain mirage that no one owns
unless quitting everything.

We are late, Heraclitus.
The Ozama of doubt, crosses and conquers
the Hudson of an urgent caress.

In the middle of that ancient river,
I found the beginning of the poem,
the last word about the dessert of time.
At the beginning of the dream
that hidden river, being born out of
rocky coasts, scraps of the dead and children.
That secret that severely dampens any geometry,
airy verse that unsuspicious questions bring,
the inappropriate notes that are too obvious,
suppressions of a body in the darkness that
ends in a smell of fish: entrance conflict,
home of the poem your hands already sweaty
from thinking about death at that time o'clock
where nothing is discovered.

You sleep
I write to kill boredom

we arrive at that port
we set sails from there with sweaty hands
and the direction we head to does not exist
river that speaks tongues that converge in an eye
space for suspicion,
river of eyes, hair,
chest within lost streams
excess
no utensils
disembarkment of illusions.

You take nothingness
your eyes, meditation of turbid water,
syllabic insistence.

Like a castaway's yawn
the habit of looking at you
from what is not written
dream
moon where the lost count their steps.

Erased notebook
foreign where languages are misleading
lips that torment a fish
raw bites, blissful frontier.

That black and white in the remote corner
where ships perish,
the end of this absurd idea of not wanting to leave
spoken body
hearsay of a goodbye, I still haven't finished
the fleeting breathing water that drains you.

The afternoon and its free lions
scarce punctuality
that dream at the shady time of transfers.

That river shall always
be the time of joy and oblivion.

Coffee at 149th

No one writes the poem.
The text just lacks the nerve,
it won't be glad about its anger.
Irresponsible presentation,
here the characters play witnesses
to an inconfessable crime,
rogues, crazy people who analyze life seriously,
ghosts that hide in a book of lies and suspicion.

Even more so the few suicide victims curse
themselves for not crossing 149th.
Others reread their mortuary notes with passion.
They all lack heroic biographies.
No one tries to read that page without falling
into one of their curses
their aura is that man who reads his truth,
the newspaper with the latest deaths
No one will talk about him
no pronouns will be evidence
for the genocide of rhythm
simply the one who suffers,
a reality full of need
unnecessary images in accordance
with that young lady who truly believes
in being yoga
or rereading a poem by Lautréamont.

Now I think of a wish, making justice to melt idiocies on the most
celebrated symbol of the empires, to spit until my stomach leaves
my body over the walls of prestige, business
cards, rhetoric awarded by ignorance.

This line is for an assumed end
no one accepts the risk
I have paid for the cold of the last six years
with trifles; summers have been a failure.
Fuck their little smiles!

This page is the gravestone for evil mothers-in-law
for virgins that call on God during masturbation
so He reads the poem of evil, divine commerce.

Oh, poets,
leave them to madness
their compromise is a vain confession
there will be no excuses
no one will correct galleys
in this reproachable poem;
its author has set a restraining order
against loan sharks and mestizos
taken by surprise by the hallucinogens
of their worries.

The call of its anonymous author terminates
the act for lack of quorum at a precise time
of a day that was never in the calendar.

Mount Hope

I shall never know if the time I spent
on *Mount Hope* was closer to hell.

Heaven, the other side of the sea
purgatory conceived on purpose
useless sun at the beginning
or end of words only thought of.

Time of not knowing if you are there
if we specify the final condition of living.
At the beginning of this word still not thought of,
Mount Hope was only the hell where we fought,
a worn-away belt on the third stair
where nothing but you stretches its rainy shape.

I shall never know if I existed between two verses of the illegible
poem within that infinite contradiction between two songs,
                    noisy and happy.
Spiritual masturbation where Saturday
is exactly the same as a remote Sunday.
In that goodbye, traced in the wall of lament,
That hand copied until praise.
Like an unkissed cheek,
Mount Hope is only a music box for some crazed exiles.
Those who spy on the reading of tears,
a surprise box dropped to the sea
by God's mistake.

In the end, these overthought
syllables shall create
—like every stupid thing said or meant—

deniable logic: the suspicion
of the infinite being that does not inhabit us
and it shall be thought from one tooth
to the other, to throw it to that rat
that reads my poems in a hallway.

If I say goodbye, I shall have faked
the end of the poem or its absence.

THE IMMIGRANTS' NOTEBOOKS (II)

In some Bronx street, New York, 1993

Translated by Lucía Ayelen Vallaro.

Body notoriety

All notoriety is an act of perversion.
Your hands get perverted in my body,
the limitless nudity gets too close to the light
and sometimes blinds the eyelid.

Runaways in the poem, you and me,
encountering the body of the image
that moves away, living on particles,
fragmented molts. A remote perversion
to look at one other, your ineffable
presence reconciles the loss of time.

The heroism of appearing suddenly expires
and leaves traces of stones, cemeteries
and compromises always in vain

The notoriety of your hair burdens me
filling the city with nonsense;
I confess my anxiety gets lost in my ankle,
empty speeches deafen me,
that demonstration of promises,
that absent rhythm and the desire
to name us ruins me
—vacuity of searching in the shadow.

A realistic love promotes falsities
that have nothing to do with pleasure.

I walk after the traces you leave,
go along the path, ruins of a cursed city,
                              refuge of tyrants
By showing you the image is erased

and another perversion is born.

Your caresses saved a disaster;
in its falsehood a monster was born,
the flowers of a comedy germinated,
a profound return translates
its tormented hives into fires.

In every perversion there is a hidden navel,
an inverted word, an escape that recycles
doubts... embezzlement of errors.

Finding repetitions or a sudden, fleeting death
like letting oneself be undressed or dying
without knowing that one is born somewhere else.

I love *that* death, for it perverts the dream.

In this, nothing weighs, not even the breasts.
The organs begin to live their own simulation,
their infinite return;
they lose their terrible anatomy
        —and pervert time.

April gardens, murals

April plants flowers on our pain and sometimes
gardens lose audience, because the day flourishes
upon death—those lips we suddenly yearn for blossom
over a metal's vapor.

Admittedly, every day a flower invades thought
oblivion germinates on the walls where men
have planted a face, the impression to be talking
from the walls with a stranger who stops by fading assertions.

Wall, flower of loneliness where we abandon thoughts;
always eternal and blurred, I wait for the day of its fall
                                        —to crack in our hands.

Gardens of the avenue

I went to see flowers at Grand Concourse
and have kept the sprouts.
I let my feet descend over the abyss
of a suicidal happiness, and suspect
that over my head there are stars.
April unleashes trees of joy where
we shall not die; there we shall leave our marks
bound to the greed of these gateway cowboys,
with no compass, tribes of the last grist.

We shall sail for chess pieces,
merchandise reborn over the void.
The body explodes, filling the universe
with our tatters, convinced that some land
shall be the orchard of our dream
or the sordidness of a love that will always
flourish upon a careless music
or sprout in the smoke of a false victory.

Reclined body

Naked on the edge of time,
cast into the void, determined,
confused to send a thought that closes the lips,
yielding, stumbling on his hands
revitalized in waiting, she softens, closes her eyelids
(dried up, bewildering, understood)
she gently circumvents a renounceable time,
leaving her left breast over the edge of the page
and opening herself; he shuts her out,
opposing, for eternity—her body confirms itself.

He gets angry, bites her body, returns an eye,
the ultimate blindness; she blurs and he vanishes.
She daunts with bitterness her keel, fading, famished.
He saves her, makes her come back, instills in her
that secret liquid that makes her live.
She pierces into him, hacks her way inward, screaming,
unleashing chains; her kisses weld them together...
exposed like a body devoured by the sea.

A woman takes care of the world

The lady takes me out
to see the sun on this particular day.
The lady makes me walk in
a predetermined direction, nervous system
creaking behind my dark circles.

I have seen it happen once again, carpeting paradises, very sunny,
sunbathing on Monday, and on the seventh day, a reverse and
blurry page, taking care of herself like a Cinderella
who needs to walk, without letting her mother rot;
smoking makes her unraveling udder soak, let it tear like Tuesday.

If she doesn't take me out like a *chula*, she hasn't seen the day
complete, the fire of going for a walk, jealous, and I caught her
looking at the sun
in the front while I feel it flickering in my temples,
on the shore, where it seems to me
that it is very good and I accept
to soak myself freely and give me out to the beginning of summer.

In that capricious extremity,
she takes me out to invent a story
or an orgy, clarity always reconciles
a corpse with that side-pear of day,
freedom of fresh grapes, for that discomfort
I feel like a vegetable, too dressed to speak
of fresh fruits or vegetables,
very bright in the afternoon, reverse,
stops in front of any wall,
a man is covered with bars,
filthy elevators and graffiti, then hairdressers,
then we return in the dark, when the young day
perishes in the horns or in the metallic shine of the light.

Female legacy

When you follow in the footsteps of a woman,
you inherit her absence, sore eyes, tears of others,
the possibility of rain, hugs,
you earn a sudden, very brief death,
                      a disdain for torture.

When surprise releases its contradictions,
the leisure of an umbrella, its lost gaze,
vain ulcers. Sometimes love invites you to fall head over heels,
fall into the delicious palm of her hands,
when it ceases to be a map, city or desert
between two fronts, intelligent flight,
bird migration and pulses of a suicide that dies
within an unspeakable happiness.
Love that runs out, restless body, rope,
destiny with the sea, dream
and that corner with traces of certain glances,
a duel with the day occurs in that angle attacked
by a weighing circle where each step accentuates
a punctuation, god's lonely writing,
unknowns that reveal their ultimate truth.

Rope, fountain where there is a smell of fish,
humidity of that fish that jumps on the heart
of an indifferent woman,
whose search concludes in *cafeterías*,

by kissing her we have inherited her smoky smile,
her nakedness with the sea when crossing in front of her
a contradiction with the course of that flight,

47

the wings that fill the avenue of the gaze,
that smile where a love that lives
is born in the hinges,
at the beginning of certain words.

By loving her, the low flights cease,
and that smell that permeates crying;
a dove flies absurdly over
the corpse of a child,
until it runs across the eyelid
that divides the city from your body,
besieged by those shallow kisses and
for that look that permeates him,
unscathed, wasteful, vaporous,
under the surprise of enemies
who write before launching a missile,
there, possibly, you are caressed
by a traitor, a deserter, or a poet
who has been expelled from paradise.
You will have the urge to dream
and that edge that draws a body
after that cold war, where the poem fails.

Contrasts

I love you just because
you love me. Because why not?

Ignorance,
the repetition ruins the sign,
and the opposite founds images,
that is why you walk away from me.
You call me because the most
beautiful game consists in playing
with fire and putting it out
when everybody inhales the smoke
—a game full of indifference, vain madness.

I love you perhaps for that ignominy,
pain that does not work anymore,
unable to continue; better to restart the poem
for that bet which shall never happen,
the politics of the sign
and your hands no longer interested.

You were the city,
sea that already befell, joy that does not
capture a dream, the pain
and that inexplicable inconsistency
of not rejecting seduction.

It will happen, but you reject
a mistake
or you suddenly doubt the right choice.

We could never find a city of trinkets,
lustful visits; the absurd guided our steps towards

a cold text when the ardor summed up untenable sentences.
You were fighting for the word that would not come out,
for the sign and its glory,
and it seemed to you that death established
the numerous landscapes of lovers situated
on a train. You sometimes rejected the port's residue
taken to exhaustion and would have liked to kiss a memory,
from the ledge where they would always
bombard our love or perhaps just the photograph of that burning.

Cowardice
to let it all come down to Somalia and those lovers who
find in the herbs a repeated, unconscious death.

To love you or lose you, to forget again and again the affirmations
where politics culminate in iodine, sneaking in without a
backpack, noisy radios in the armpits of a suicide that cannot
interrupt the wings of this thought, the most lucid fasting
and that desire to leave, perhaps exactly the same as returning.

You began on the sad side a joy that strips you
and ended with a stubborn sensation of not being able
to settle for a traditional way of loving, fleeing to the unnecessary
side, finding faith in the useless, an indispensable goodbye,
happiness too contagious to repeat.

Sometimes, forgiveness bothers with a caress,
Vain illness, the humor is to look for you where the castaway
disinherited his breath and freedom foretells a voluntary
suicide, neither lie nor error, zeal, truth,
            —distrust always those words.

What we are left with in the end

In the end
we are left with that intention of astonishment.
We enjoyed a precocious peace that unraveled
in a hinge where a rusty hero sleeps, symbol of
a continuous struggle with death

Sunny day, Sunday, our feet are bumpy and
we kick -disenchanted- the flowers, an invisible bush,
a day with lions, avenues and your hands,
marbles like a degradation of the dream continue escaping,
awakening niches, caverns of fury, that peace we cultivate
with two hands, a woman who, after giving her body
on behalf of mine has found an indifferent peace.

I agree with someone: the hero is dead,
the discourse of his feats creates famine,
disdain that we hurry in a suspicious cigarette.

Your sweat, my hands, your unknown hair
that curiosity to make war on you since that tomorrow,
since that goodbye that survives the encounter with the other.

We eternalize an anxious ash,
unprolongable being, you look at me like a Somali,
with that thirst that does not cease when the hero
draws an afternoon, a dream, empty amphora
where the warrior carries his pills, perhaps a cigar,
simple peace, a photo taken when you take your shoes off
and then my heart dies whipped with shame, in that anguished
kiss that we both enjoyed on a Friday, from a song that makes our
love survive, dream or trap that never gives a bird's sign,
in fish or in some lotus flower,
you look up at me, beautiful lie, pain besieged
by fog, simple ideology of the two.

Peace, that parted lip, inflexible index finger
and the disobedience of taking the word,

domains of smoke, fences,
hair where a sea borders eyes,
springs, granite benches and braids.

A freedom worked on the sand that we will never
set foot on, words from a remote city where
we agreed to leave. It is there where love is,
in the lost game, where the naked players disappear,
without any dice, no orchid from that archeology,
useless childishness, turning over a spinning top.
From that millenary collapse I look at you, inexplicable,
like the absolute being that speaks for a city
where the sea always gnaws keels, stones, gazes,
and that thought kiss, written on the water, like oblivion.

SUBWAY
LIVING UNDERGROUND AND OTHER CONFESSIONS

(New York, 1999)

Translated by Lucía Ayelen Vallaro.

Procedure

In order not to welcome a recurring
vocabulary, we returned to cleanliness,
racism or nationalism.

God approves an amnesty for those
who continue as prisoners in the subway,
especially for those who sleep their best nap
on the bench waiting for death or on the doorstep awaiting our
final wish, without flowers
and without the chocolates of a memory.
Reform approved for those who live between
the bars of a stormy futile career, hunched
over a newspaper or excited to sip beers
that have triumphed over a regret.
These prisoners must occupy the underground
for a week of summer relaxation.
It is urgent that they experience a strange sense
of freedom and rediscover the sweetness of putrefaction.

Evening load

We go with our remains of the day, with the hours lost on the rails of time. There is an error that rolls towards the void and our worn shoes from waiting in vain for a wagon where new loads will come, satisfied men, surrounded by masked men bring umbrellas and women sew up their belongings in the open air. The legs will seek the pleasure of other gazes or will guide themselves towards an absurd door, where other men will hide heads empty of questions, melted on pieces of other bodies. Eye reflexes return, abandoning noises. Towns that will never again see the light of day will descend
—the ladder to another inhabitable city.

The machinist

After locating him at the ends of the train car,
I have observed him open his safe, the train going nowhere
or at a standstill, with the doors of the world wide open,
stretching, uttering a deep sigh, or keeping his cabin door ajar,
breathing or looking for the air that has disappeared.

We know that it is him because of his wide glasses,
made to discover bugs or avoid sudden blindness.
I have noticed that machinists lose many things over several years
of running through the tunnels. Sometimes they leave their
mansion door, the size of a body and half a chair, to stand
at the doors, catching those who urinate on an avenue,
or the smokers that defy death in the path of those
who run away from the train car to look for someone lost,
who cannot find himself, either running along
the nine between-doors, as if chasing keychains,
battery sellers, the beggars emigrate from the city,
 change stations and desires, relocating to another
                              —zone of exclusion.

Many times, the Subject plays to be seen.
He wants to be caught and remains
for a long time looking at the end of the train car he deems
to command. He wants to take a break from his chamber
and stretch his legs to flirt with the traveler's normality.
The man strolls around with the key to the train,
                         —prepared for anything.

Today it occurred to him to let the "E" roll towards the abyss,
when he and his friend disagree. A pair of iguana eyes look into
the horizon. If the temperature rises, the tenants open their coats,

57

abandon their legs and lie carelessly, ready for anything.
They leave an inviting umbrella on the bench.
They get rid of their bags or deafened radios
and get carried away by the machinist who has already
fled into a tunnel where hope does not exist.

After a table of earrings

When I head towards the blue circle
where they have locked the capital letter that throws us
to the city's edge, we enter among the waiting
men and women. We have not agreed to meet,
to wander around, but their satisfaction to see me again is evident,
for they have diverted their look. I flee from their gaze to the detail
of a fragmented body, severed towards a line in the conversation
of a visitor from the other city. Or we choose the land
of involuntary embraces or genitals inadvertently shown
with hands carelessly drooping, while the others
(or that who seemed distant) cling to the rails
or the colossal bars of an involuntary crucifixion.

Heads, apparently free, tilt towards a book that
the train betrays, or that beautiful and indifferent eye stares
over an unfathomable line, and the noises have revived
the concentration in this new gravity that swings towards
a pendulum, making the feet converse, or unbinding the ankles,
they think more than our hand or our newspapers, sometimes
causing love to throw them to our footsteps' dust.

Curse on the rails

How to destroy this misery if we have stumbled upon a strange
pronoun, or hear how they consume syllables, evening hair, lips...

We look for bodies covered with antiques, stains, piercings
or naked-down-to-their-twilight pubes. Later they melted
and never looked up to hear the maracas, accordions, mechanized
barks going towards the driver's cabin, to the doorways
between train cars where we never wanted to smoke or split
the cars where other cities were, other dreams that went
forward or stepped back towards others that, maybe,
ignored the involuntary arrival of masked hearts,
painted faces and women that come in with their makeup artists
or their dogs, for security reasons or in virtue of some hypnotic
                                        —effect of the noise.

THE PERFUME OF BOWLING GREEN

(New York, 2001)

Poeticus Eficacciae

Translated by Carolina Bonansea.

Palestine

If I were to love another woman,
I would call her Palestine. I would hug her around
Jerusalem. In a bastion in Gaza, we would save the sea.
We would hide again at the edge of Egypt;
nobody would know.
We would make love plenty of times
on the debris of Jenin, naked as the first lovers
in the myth; we would create apples or maybe mangoes.
The serpent would come out from the first kiss
to conjure a new attack.

We would say the Apache simply drew the setting
of an orgy, but they would call it Palestine many times.
Perhaps the arrogance of the wall has only made me
love you more; naturally, there would not be enough
space to alleviate the knees, heal the wounds,
place offerings on a bombed garden.

I would say she calls me anyways, when the sun sets,
at the end of a bloody battle, after everything calms
down. I will walk down your debris again,
the fragments of a morning that bursts destroying
wishes, the pieces of an irrevocable goodbye,
of a delayed embrace over the outline
of a moon spilling onto the day.

It is still fixed, indifferent like the brother's god,
that is to say: the Cain that wants to be David
or the Goliath, that endures in the Hudson, suspicious,
like the one you invoke every time you decide to depart
toward the hereafter; and you do it without interrupting

those that fill the day with the pleasure to live,
who can still taste a routine while you come back
in a hurry to the old Trojan horse.

You return, little by little, to the autumn of the stones,
to that sand that we have not been able to enjoy.
War has become personal and, if you die, I will also
cultivate the joy of an indifferent moon, to forget
that there is still oxygen left, convinced
that you will live, that one day you will escape
the missile, the wing of an invisible plane.

They can't prevent us from kissing each other,
dipping our ankles in that millenary river of time,
tasting the fingertips of this love against
the waters of this broken day to count crags, toy's dust,
talc and disdain; and those things that were there since
yesterday, when the brother would share water,
wind and sand from the same desert, the insects
that walk across without asking for permission
                        —to occupy your hands.

If there is any trace left

Is there any space left for frankness?
Is there any room among our domestic
chores for something that is not part
of a shady deal? The deserters chose something
healthier: to abandon pencils, notes, hopeless drafts,
letters, senseless albums, new technologies;
to make way among the lies,
the footnotes, the aided contempt
of the self. We would have focused on hiding pronouns,
on destroying adverbs, on demolishing courtesy phrases
and other priceless nonsense
because we ignore on which side the neighbor sleeps.

I elude the miracle of a premeditated abortion,
when this blessed civilization was bleeding out.
To be frank, if persuasion continues dragging greed,
the coward exhibitionism of something that still allows
us to pick up garlic heads, onions that commanded
revenge, the fruits could contradict orders, memories.
Maybe they saved the touch of an evil memory
to then recompose what was coming, to avoid
the outline of those who spread joy, to look at
the aggressor hiding in the phrases of a puzzle,
mutinied against the one saying them out loud,
simply because it stinks.

He put back on the table new aggressions,
contempt for those who trust in incoherence;
maybe I could have defended my morality,
another word devoured by those in uniform.
They believe they have the right to decide

the wrong way I followed when I avoided the fear.
I've said it before: we refuse to obey, to keep the secret
of the next Holocaust. I only wanted to have some
baggage, an eye that helped other fallen men to see.

An emptier land would attract delicious curses.
It would open the way for the next David,
turbid and random, too positive, trusting tomorrow.
Every day it sleeps in somebody else's bed,
with bloodstained hands, being able still to send flowers,
or call for people to discover that it no longer exists,
it can kiss its contemporaries and every day
                    —destroy their memory.

Mundane diaspora

To many victors, the best trade
in the world would consist in leaving everything right
where it is, shutting up, avoiding public statements,
slipping away graciously among those who don't want
to confront their destiny, becoming cowards with
a bottle of wine in their hands, applauding those
who swear before God's cards, cautiously going
to their daily jobs, without admitting that we're still
there, and that the others are still silent, managing
a couple of hours of misery, pills hidden inside
suspicious backpacks, tasting a bit of fate, dancing,
following the way from the day before with the passion
of a disguised angel in front of the enemy's board,
jealous to fill the trash with cigarette butts that
germinate in the dark. Walking on such a secret day,
we had not had a day like that.
The trade of living a positive life is still delirious.
We seduce others with the idea of an identity
that doesn't really fit us; as a protest, we showed a
personal object to the public—they had celebrated
that gesture before, had discarded that vulgarity,
that desire to be talked about.

We will get through, and new oaths appeared,
little flags, tiny certifications, a couple of hours would
make a difference, we would simply have to burn
newspapers to stop being questionable.
There is no reason to be like those who still recognize
the usefulness of a psychologist or a friend
who discovers how ignorant we were when we turned
up the volume on the TV, spoke out loud and left out

the idea of us being children.

Something stank but they convinced us it didn't.
Look for that perfume and that juice that won't stop our
thirst on the other side of the sea, the silenced error,
the caresses that started a discussion; maybe we worried
too much about Janet Jackson's withered womb,
or about a flag brushing against Madonna's pubis
or covering badly shaved heads, succulent bosoms,
legs or inexplicable desires for a brother that no longer
existed, who didn't have to defend neither his color
nor his vanity or the guilt of the accusers.

We were not judges or Messiahs or soldiers, we left out
of every discussion those who executed, beyond the sea,
other people who had hairs, heads and dreams,
the same way as those buried in mass graves and even
the relentless judges, for now it's better if you keep
going, turn right and forget about it, neither the weapon
of the crime nor the soldier that eats every day in a table
with flowers where there are children and maybe
grandparents and plans to come back to normalcy
                            —are under discussion.

The new face of the tyrant

Dressed as a civilian, flawless, not as thin as his victims,
one day he comes back to his dog, and you see him
hugging it with affection in front of
the cameras, imitating a soldier on leave.

He takes 15 days off to go back to his father and mother
and the rest of the dynasty members. Today, he looked
for the lethal weapons under his bed.
He played shameless again, pretended to be a magician
who fails to keep his promises. They weren't under
the furniture, and he even tried to take his wallet out
and prove that he did not have any perverse motifs;
he tried to pretend he was incorruptible and failed
                                        —even harder.

The guardians were hidden so the people wouldn't see
them, and, by the way, nobody knows if he voted or was
made to believe he was voting for these men who were
brothers in arms, with distant bravery, discreet to shed
the blood of their enemies, lovers of the color green
because of forgotten environmental reasons,
and of that green that's hard to replicate
and that doesn't buy everything, only those
who voted to find a boy who emulated the father
and who went beyond, who showed the most cowardice,
the most disdain for those who were barefoot
and for the clergymen who threatened democracy
that secretly failed, the one still hidden on the planes,
peacefully sleeping in the aircraft carriers
and in the phrases without obstacles, swear words
and gestures that emerge in the presence of the peace

cries, in all the councils where, not so long ago,
he accepted a slave who was wrong, a simple
intelligence mistake that won't bring upon a *Watergate*
nor a magistrate's court where his friends would kiss
him on the cheek. He forgot about history,
it was a simple honesty crisis, the oblivion
of the colonized, the child of the woman in labor,
of the black woman who now applauds
this new white man, the islander who forgot that,
once, he was smuggled in,
to support the tyrant determined
to free the world of uncomfortable turbans,
ugly Levites and hats that don't reveal the oblivion,
that don't hide the determination to resist the tyrant
that, today, by the way, cried, prayed, and talked about
baseball, and yearned for the son that didn't come in
time, in the moments when the slave was writing
the constitution and the architects were designing
the country that was promised to the massacre.

ODDYSSY OF TIME

(New York, 2005)

Translated by Carolina Bonansea.

Epitaphs

When, from some ghetto, other heroes shoot
on the leagues, those who fast over a body, the last one,
the suicidal from last night, then, you run away
and hide in a park, behind the sunflowers,
under the candles and the silent angels, and all because
the socks won't help neither your long legs nor your
damaged ankle breaking now, right when you were
hoping to float, or at least doing it until another corpse
showed up on the crystal clear water of that river that
you can't see or that sea you announce, saying it was
possessed by you, imprisoned in a simple seashell
hidden in a room, riddled with white angels and flowery
tablecloths —the same flowers you planted when you
ran away from one of those factories that make it
possible to believe you're alive, that you will save
the day with a revenge made of sunflowers or candles
stagnant on fake water, while you breathe, or think
you're doing so, on a sofa that is floating, tilting towards
a crystal that barely reproduces silhouettes.

The mischievous masts are impressive, spied by a faint
light that silver-plates torsos, paintings that strip
the existence from deep signs, shadows or tapestries
where, emphatically, those flowers reappear from
the end, which is no longer as simple nor as lucky as it
used to be, those arrogant and rude days that ignited
their frenzy over streets with replicas, with nice curtains
to decorate those absent afternoons, that wind that
cannot crash with the trees which don't foretell a thing,
not even another spring driven by some melody,
those which were and barely are reasons to stop in
another time, throwing water to the wind, filling socks
with colors and reducing glutei for a glamor
that seems to have reached its end.

73

Disarmed woman

If they have disarmed you, what will you invent
to try and float? To move forward towards
a log, to make a phone call and let the night
be an infinitive that germinates every two seconds
with a restless disdain, and all because you didn't
know how to hide in the trenches and cry, holding
children, combs or lipsticks or, a menstruation
drill that happened with more burning heat,
in the instant when someone, a client, a friend,
an immigrant stabbed in the back, and who didn't
stop the fears from coming, the desire to escape
for a couple of hours and just float, because
an immigrant, even though they know how
to swim, can only float over flowers or ribbons
or garments that would light up a trench where
you won't ever be. You would have come to offer
the faithful and delicious day of naked egos,
the simulations that start with words, these
umbrellas or bubble gums or sticks adrift, good
to float over the doubts, not knowing that,
without thinking, we shoot toward remote seas
that don't go out, that don't ask questions
and work a discarded day, filled with music,
with the sister I dreamt of having, or the father
that should have been my son, or the friend
that should have been my brother who, however,
becomes words that devour the bodies,
words that float only over avenues taken by other
furtive hunters, by other bathers spotlessly
dressed, who float on their suits,
with their champagne glasses, with their cheese
that inquire about an answer and dissolve their
pretentiousness over penetrating perfumes
that make the necks float with more urgency
toward the shore of these colorless endings.

Riding the 6

Now we can finally piss on the previous day.
A few hours after being emotionally moved
by that yesterday which, however, could be
a discarded today, divided in small bits of perhaps,
or extremely simple maybes, left behind
by the determination to make circles around our
own desire to know what happened, where
that memory of days planted on recollection went,
celebrated or cursed, leaving the sea behind,
getting far away from the 'we coulds', and think
the night is still an extension or that deal of seeing
the glass fall, the last seconds drunken on wishes,
promises and plans that would fail again, schemes
that would give in to the gentleness of being, to its
persistence in drawing back curtains to mumble
stuff; we would come renewed of gluttonous
questions and dreams destroyed by a thought,
when the endings exploded in the confinements,
gave in to the old plan to court the gods.

Go and curse those who would be the heroes
of a new suffering, those who toasted for twelve
months, their fists held firm or their fingers
erected, and broken glasses under the arrows
that underline the growths that do not contain us,
that predict an empty and suffocating progress,
only little bells arriving, priests, moneylenders
and that smoke that changes the smell of those
who tend to calculate how much they will eat
during the year, opening spaces for the new
melons, for the minutes that won't give back the
water beds, the fatherless sentries,
the childless mothers pushing the boats, carrying
the fish that won't multiply on the tables
of the following dinners with smiling apostles that,
once again, destroy the compasses, kissing

an empire's ass or seducing those who haven't
been able to try their first toothpaste yet, those
who swim mercilessly following a heart that sails.

They float, with no shark of a momentary
happiness arriving at the extended gardens,
postponed by fasting or fatuous desires
to go out to a different era.

We have only segregated particles of life,
ideas that weren't presented on time and which,
however, were left behind, or returned to those
who follow us, pretending the same sun won't
come back, nor the same moon
nor the unbearable disdain with those monsters
annoyed by your hands, jealous of your fingers
that do not sing, that do not work the upcoming
crime with the apathy of yore, when those jealous
merchants desired you from those box seats,
those who always deserve to notice
the enthusiasm with which we should divide
the next-to-last morning, the kisses and the strokes
that brought back the same, the joyful one that,
once again, loses his mind because of a lipstick,
or a pair of socks that won't hurt as much as
expected nor will they give birth to more *noes*
or more *whats*, and gloomy ardors from a god
that does not want us to make love in such a hurry.

First impressions

Why not remember the first sigh, the first time our
lips cursed? If they kissed or succumbed on a body
that was just asking.

We could make a note of the tempestuous clitoris
that no longer turns on the cold nor causes
the heat announced by the season. We should step
out and touch things for the first time. It should be
allowed, once and for all, to kill the one who
crossed paths with the same desire, to have fun
from nothing, from the null point of all
misfortunes, or that field where we are not,
to begin from that absence that gravitates over
the desire to be free for the first time,
ready to obey the only true law, the one law that
comes from the will that hasn't been tarnished
nor noticed in books nor suspected by a stripped
line,   a room reopened and curtains burnt,
saturated desire, the body defeated by those old
stenches, licked by drunk judges, magistrates
that come from us with the sapience of a planet
falling and collapsing on the hands of the chained
ones and the hypocrites, and all the wicked ones
that would melt our hearts with new absurdities.

ECHOES OF THE DIASPORA ARK

(New York, 2008)

Translated by Carolina Bonansea.

Fictional resignation letter to the Dominican Culture Commission in the US, year 2008

If I were given the honor to act for my
audience, ready for joy, naked, awake,
barefoot, revealing my pantyhose and my
sheer socks for an audience that applauds,
kneels or crowds around before the wrecked
busts or looks at the empty walls
or the windows plagued with mythologies,
that invisible window, anonymous,
as everything we do, I would say the
following, and I would keep my discretion
as if a bureaucrat who eats punctually
or brings their host to *Requena* to eat with
the dead in a sweet, memorable banquet.

Here are the gestures of this preterit.

It was this comedy's Lentini who never arrived.

Sometimes I was myself in my fucking ambiguity
or tried to be; a lot of times, when singing was not
for me, but for those who come when they think
they're coming or who, when they leave,
suspect they are coming
or have left in the wrong direction.

The joyful niche of the room has been the haven
of peace, the theater of happiness,
the casual shadow of a useless revenge,
that sand without blood and without erect limbs
destroyed for a feast of repentant dinner with

authoritarian gifts, white envelopes and repressed
silences; and since there are no ships or planes,
not even rafts, there weren't any white flowers
planted nor paddles on the waves of this afternoon,
left to its fate, demolished by the sapience afflictions
or the frames installed to suppress a desire or to chase
after the suspicion of a memory. I haven't been invited
by fate to watch the descent of this clod condemned
to its joy, imposed to the disdain of the universal
applause, to trace the circumference of a genius idea,
of these misplaced anniversaries or this barren season,
when we could have been *us*, we were someone else,
the cremated ones under the twilight
the holy pope or the libertarian altar boys from a sigh
we inaugurated words of thanks or the tenderness
of goodbye, with no arms raised in the manly way
of Brother Antón Montesinos or hugs drawn on a paper
thrown away on a wet street.

I have been perfectly the one on Mondays or neutral
Saturdays. Anyone would have sworn I have been
the one on the indecisive Wednesday of regular
clothing, hugs caressed by the crowd, feeling he was
a part of a verse he thought or a phrase never
                              —pronounced in public.

The libertarian orgy dies between these clean and white
walls where someone separates chairs or measures
distances. Between them, there is a historic thought;
the slave ate the bread or gave away his smile
to the thieves crucified by the fullness.

Someone ran away through the back door,
leaving a message in the darkness of the dressing room

where the culture of a nominal country was being
painted and the demons of the greedy apathy were
being born—the cursed breath of an unfortunate
evening, painted for the most patriotic tenderness
in the world, thankful for those who already thought
                                    —about their absence.

We were those pantomimes, those considerate goblins,
even though the Hispanic and oligarch city wouldn't tell
on us, the politicians dominated the scenery of another
madhouse, while going over the walls, obsolete since
the extermination the faces of the fallen would strip
and the *Great Zodiacal Room*,
the *Great Hall of the bittersweet dead*
loomed over their guarded regret and, one day,
Christ the Redeemer arrives, hidden in a bolero.

To compensate the heroines, reverends were postulated,
eyes were closed, hearts were opened, tempered
by the distance, culture was made, flags were hidden
under lock   and key, then the auditor would come,
the invisible financial health inspector
and the good reader of the ruined volts.

Dirty rags were washed,
in another time, something would activate
in our hearts, regretful of eating plenty,
good to belittle the great work,
the social work of the blessed goodbye
without repressing any fondness
nor any will to be terrifyingly punctual.

What's the point of announcing the imperious sex,
the lucid background? Slavery has been refuted by the

slogans. A celebratory wind fills the beautiful big thing
of the *Requena* with furious mothers in yet another
clarity crisis, with books thrown to the crowd,
and the horror spelled. And never just like now,
the exile brags about its victories;
boasts about banished letters and clean History.

It stands out among the darkness of the hit men,
represented by some Aladdin's extinguished lamp.

Those who suspected a way of moving their hands
are now free; they were dismissed in the exercise
of their own will. Precious debts gravitated
in the contemplation of the saltpeter and the purity
inaugurated the value of a slow goodbye, returning
to the crime hurrying the hands, crossing the eyebrows
and with the beautiful script of the *Great Terror Room*
under the armpit, the mantle of the great scenery
dropped its blouses. It opened up its *Victoria's Secret;*
the belly didn't hide any more tenderness
nor an enthusiast belly button among the editorials.
The great prize of the exiled letters gave birth to sensual
balls, administered the death certificates of the dissident
dreamers, a cultural tourism of committed national
juries, so other despicable suicide victims choked us off
when the charitable shit entered, shameless,
in the *Requena*, and the sacred names in the imported
                                        —altar jumped.

The vegetarian *ciguapas* pronounced the strange
alphabet of a car, our people regret their true identities,
ran with gratitude, jumped in pieces when they
discovered the rain of another innocence
or stepped on a torment snow, under the celebrated

plunder they were descending down on Amsterdam
Avenue; it was a redeeming nationalism, without stairs
or shyness in their cheeks, there were skirts missing,
not men, as Pedro Mir said in order to denounce
the chill of a phallic heat, pants jumping to unknit
brows, windows to see the runaway cars
from the windows, the men couldn't cry their childhood,
better to shut up like traitors and wait for the freedom
of the owners of the modern estate,
waiting for the slave secret with poetic buttocks just like
the rumor of cinnamon or the scented tea leaves
make the lips go crazy and that smell keeps sheltering
in the congested noses. We still breathe the scent
of a Santo Domingo coffee or some tea painted
in the paper cups, questioned from a redeeming
corner, good for plotting against the camera's
old gestures of freedom discovered.

I was free.
I don't know if I was ever free from me,
from everyone else.

This impersonal pronoun has been seen and felt
by the cameras; this *I*, as useless as the *us*
from immediate involvement
or the daily *hurakiris* on the snow.

It has been related to the plans, has been a part
of a History full of grandiloquence.

Lentini didn't quit because he was slandered.
I have been recognized. I can't complain about my luck
of the pages that stood up to tell me: "Hello, Lentini,
I haven't been the only fool in the movie

nor the sick one who laughed; not even the perfumed
monster described by the massacre that eats
the *Requena* when everyone else has left."

I have been me, him, that one, those, the same.

I've been the one eating the saliva and vomiting
my attributes. I've been the one taking off the make-up
without being the woman from Friday,
the one that arrives at six o'clock
or leaves to see Amsterdam Ave. one last time.
I haven't been the light-skinned *Ciguapa* named Uber,
as the paradise of survival of poetry in the world
nor the poet who raised the flag of an honest Duterte,
nor the one who flew as a miserable Superman,
looking for the right words for the satrap or fresh water
for the kneeling *clod* to kiss,
the virgin's cheeks or discover
the naked ankles of indifference.

The afternoon and its notebooks opened fire
against boredom. The slogans vanished
and we made room for goodbye; the ship left.
We quenched the History's shipwreck survivors' thirst
where I have been well paid, seated, keeling, so God
won't disturb the happiness of those who leave
with the suspicious truth about whether I did or didn't
sign my disappearance order, without showing up
in the papers from June 14th, 1962, but in the *yellow pages*
of Facebook's altar, in broad daylight or nightlight.

Maybe I was just another rebel, another person forced
to sign a moratorium, another day, in the month
of the stolen flowers and the sunny afternoon booed

for an orgasm.

I honored and I was dishonored
for being outside the altar;
the priests arrived to applaud the modern dictator.

By the way, here, there has never been,
is not, and will never be reason to discuss it,
not even a real Johnny Abbes García
nor a real Lentini or a 40³ (for make-up),
not even a young Joaquín Balaguer with real common
sense, regretting the mystery of his current page.

The superstitious have been liberated,
the reggae was expelled on time and the merengue
from *El Padrino*, played all night, filling the haven
with blood; the concubines danced and the godchildren
spitted on the pizzas, posed for a cake
where there were no missing candles.

The victims missed the birthday,
celebrated in their absence,
discussed and whispered in their absence, sensed,
devoured by lights and eyes juicy questions,
affirmations of the one who left a character
in the disappeared party installed the mics,
the hidden terrorist is shaking,
nobody tells us who we are,
history is shit, now the one we're looking for is singing,
the absent poet makes room for the singer,
those in the middle are jumping in their absence,
the grapes condemned to the torture of monolingual

---

³ *La 40* was the name given to an infamous torture house used by Tyrant Trujillo's henchmen.

87

tongues the size of these reefs, God's black beans

taken care of with the skills of a mental blackout kissed
on the irreverence attempts, Job's patience cut short
by the rite of speed and the angelical stigma of the day's
antologazos, made invisible by the rot.

If there is incense and sleep, it's difficult to caress one's
cold balls, to leave offers over the buttock's sober lack
of interest, the saint's unnoticed collection boxes
the cameras know it, they can see all day, neutral,
well positioned, bare, they discovered the desire
of being caressed. They have lasted the first days,
when we believed they existed in their invisible trade,
the incredible monster with a thousand eyes,
and no brain could see the notebooks,
notice the water, exceed a tear's surface,
place itself as an innocent little popcorn,
without flies or worms, it grew within terror,
the durable shadow of the dictator on duty, a murky
atmosphere was enough to raffle an idea, to disconnect
the longing and ask for help from an upset angel,
to ask for an audience and proclaim that the vegetarian
ciguapas cannot enter, nor those who live in the window
of goodbye, the official patrician of the Count
of Peñalba's Gate of the independence lost in 1844,
who wasn't rescued nor questioned.

The city denounced the confusion of that *glamour.*
The politicians dominated the stage of another annual
madhouse, when, going through the walls
of a disposable imagination, the faces of the fallen
were stripped and the *Great Hall of Exile,*
the *Great Hall of the Dead,* in danger of waking up

from a suspicious docility,
loomed over their guarded regret;
and, one day, Christ the Redeemer arrives,

hidden in a bolero to compensate the heroines,
reverends were postulated, eyes were closed,
hearts opened, culture was made,
flags were hidden under lock and key.

The auditor arrived,
the inspector and good reader of the volts,
and the rags were washed, something was activated
in our heart, regretful of eating plenty,
good to celebrate the great work,
the social work of a despicable goodbye
without suppressing any fondness
nor its thirst to be terrifyingly punctual,
what is the point of announcing
the imperious sex... the lucid background?

Slavery has been refuted by slogans,
a celebratory wind fills the *Requena*
with furious mothers,
with books thrown to the crowd and the horror
is spelled and never just like now,
an exile brags about victories.

I still remember the last sharks
entering with the crowd
from the cultural corridor any day
in the elevators of solitude or they
would go down with no unexpected corsairs nor any
modesty in their hands, but there were no Messiahs

missing in the twilight nor any Billy goat to stretch
the legs, windows to see the cars resting
from the last runaway to the ATM
of a spectacular romance with the embarrassment,
and the innocent audience inside
the room was crying
as mischievous children in this pirate fantasy
and it was healthy to wait
for the so-called owner's freedom,
waiting for the secret of the lucid buttocks
aspiring the humor of cinnamon or the tea leaves
that wait and the smell won't stop looking
for refugee in the *Requena;*
and it's obvious we're leaving, we were,
we have been those who, some time ago, imagined
that they could burn in the notebooks, opening up
voices, tormenting the cold hardness in the cornices
and then covering the *toilet* to hide a universal smell,
in those days when passing napkins on the lips rivaled
with the nightmares of a sensual slave's prison
imagined in the Great Hall, narrated during
a Fall full of opened books and enthusiastic customers,
dressed for church when the platform to Amsterdam
was filled with liberal sanctimonious people, sexual
deviants and exiles who were shooting blunderbuss
bullets from an ideological pigeon loft,
they came here to describe the epitaph of the frames,
the lack of faces in the paintings or to deny
the reality crisis under the glass
of *the Great Window of the Motherland.*

POEMS OF
THE FIRST DAY

(New York, 2009)

Translated by Juanita Eslava Bejarano.

Wednesday celebration

Wednesday is good for rubbing your hands
and maybe shouting 'The day has come!'
The hands stop searching for the navel,
we have arrived on time,
their misery will not save us from this feeling
of keeping pianos, hiding keys,
kissing letters, delirious in the reasoning of the poem.

An hour has passed and the victims have not arrived yet.
Suicide lovers devour the sand,
feeling the grass of a cry´s splendor.
Our hands reach out, consequences circulate,
many hours of waiting await, the wounds
couldn't be postponed to Saturday.
Monday was too sorrowful to stop slandering
this invisible line, the heat behind the glasses
glimpses the wonders of the week,
slaves love him and gravediggers despise him.
Predicting a thirst for flowers, a guilty coffin
will march through the cities in search of the corpse
or maybe we will resurrect
from this Wednesday at 2 in the morning.

It could not be otherwise.
It would have to be said in a quiet voice.
Impossible things-people have lost dignity,
why hide those who die fighting
for an orchid or build walls, mortgaging
the previous caresses and flagrant words?

Tasteless this day to yet-unpaid-for, dispossessed by nature,
incorruptible, it announces the sacrilege of questions;
the waves of wine are not hidden in backpacks
and the infamy of kissing hips is not sold for less
nor is shooting pigeons toward an enemy beach.

Volunteers treasure the iniquities of this day.
Painted sunflowers predict a deranged angel
or a room where nurses masturbate the book
or maybe drop down on the pavement
looking for the right way to say goodbye
to the day on the carpets,
in the books silenced for reporting
a Wednesday divided in two, dejected
by perhaps or maybes or a colorless burning.

It flutters its sigh by asking to host an asylum
divided into invisible tiny pieces of gazes.
Observers taste the selflessness
of the minutes sold in a puny day,
good for melting the fingertips;
there lies the indifferent blue of Wednesday.

They want to erase it from the map,
vandalize it, so that their incense
does not reach the heights of this indifference or dissipate
a perfume, of notebooks repressed by the wind.

No exit

Either everything is Christian Dior or our love is false.
Nothing exists when you are gone—why say
without you if nonsense announces a drunken city
where love takes advantage of the heart
so that a pencil asks questions or curses answers.

God is a simple knowledge of you.
The skin resists, the doubts tremble,
the hands of the *yesses* warn stale cheeses,
a melody germinates its indiscreet pen
and all awakened being predicts a fight
where sleep breeds. The night saves us,
even if everything is *eau de cologne* and a scalpel.
No one would give birth here if they weren't ready
to love this body stranded between books,
dirty with ink and jealous of the wind.
The thirsty sun burns, the cold lip prints your hair.
If you didn't come to hear this song
liquefied among the streets,
winged to smash into pieces,
this rib no longer hides the seeds' moisture
nor does the heat escape between the legs.

RANDOM POEMS

(New York, 2008-2010)

Translated by Juanita Eslava Bejarano.

Suspicious certainty

If you all think there is something of you
that actually exists, please establish an entelechy to find out.

His parents don't recognize him.

Why stop to shave him or apply make-up on her,
paint a mole on her cheek, call *her*?
What does it matter if she's a number, a graffiti?
We don't know what her name was,
if she had a bicycle, chapped lips.
We saw her raise a hand
before jumping onto the genes of such colorless prosperity.

The tasteless beggars pawned a sign,
assembled a seductive pose, cleaned up the town
of pennies printed on the salt and of liar rats.
The habitual bridge was laden with red flowers
to lick the back of the absurd.

A metamorphosis inaugurated Friday's draw
and only the useless walking bodies were left free
—those who refused to be tallied by the census.
Fortunately, older women were left out
unchained by the memory of the emptiness.
Snipers of my generation
entrenched in a ghetto of dull hammers
and deaf flags waving for otherness,
those willing to shoot to kill boredom.
The insane bonded to their contempt
jump into the emptiness and those genitalia
stranded in a corner of time
waiting for a cigarette, intoxicated
by the smell that does not awaken nostalgia.

Lunch time at York College

Fear is not accidental.
It has discovered the movement of my hands.
My lost glasses assure that I was able to see
a few hours ago. Without them, precariousness fights
its last battle. The light assumes a lost residency.
It gives solidity to the body and sleaze to desire;
it establishes colors that do not dump
everything that crying gives us back.
Clarity will not allow us to love each other more
nor hate us less. Be suspicious about this sweet
feeling, it drags tenderness, consumes absence;
it is not present in the initiation
of the unsustainable body.

Fear doesn't give in to this incestuous hour.
We all see each other eating the same grapes.
The same months eat the same hours.
This second is desperate to devour its nothingness.
There are failed bodies trapped by pity.
The afternoon is splendid to jump into the emptiness,
ignore without pain the nudes of the first day of the week.
Skeptical about our irremediable presence,
now is when we start to pretend.
The myth´s night drags its jokes,
redeems chains that will come to fall on the gray ink
of the newly condemned to live in the haze
under a lamp that one day will go out forever.

Cursed spotlight

When I came out of my mother's womb,
I had a father. He came from time to time
to see me. I had the right to childhood
in bakeries. Of course, he was a Christian
—he had the right to bear a cross.
I was heterosexual per antonomasia and nature.
Even if I didn't know what that word meant.
I was entitled to a gun for three days,
to a couple of grenades designed for the game;
for the bazooka, and several bullets I found
in La Salcedo, also an eyemask, a *Red Rider* suit,
a white horse for the *Lone Ranger*, a cape,
a certain vegetable, a machine gun
                that illuminated dreams.
I had the right to dawdle the city in pursuit
of milk. I had a disease willing to caress my father's pockets,
my mother's kiosk, chickens
to feed my older brother's binges, rabbits for my cats.
I had an octopus at my service,
shiny and adult when the cement´s wealth took root.
La Vieja Belén brought me a *Paso Fino* horse.
I had white chickens, brown ones, spotted swallows,
invaders in green entering my room
taking the weapons the camels brought me.

One day, I discovered that all possession
is an illusion, including my father, my mother,
my fish... I no longer had the country without assault,
the moon without hunger;
the beaches lost their fictional dimension.

The world was falling apart like a *Cuaba*-soap bubble.
I had the right to follow the priest of the procession
to learn three words in Latin to cross myself.
I had the right to go to the cheap movie theaters.
I fully enjoyed tenant rights.

I was able to straddle the trenches,
hear gunshots, sleep on the ground,
spot the invader breaking down a toy door.

I had the right to a city taken by siege.
My laughter had the right to hope.

Learning to die

Learning to die has its secrets in humidity,
its broken ribs, the armpit stench without its juice,
and a fishing of deaf collarbones in honor of the lucid shoulder.

From a motel, dying frees the poem of other truths.
There is nothing wrong with dying for three hours
or resurrecting underwater
—sigh of this dying infamy.
The window blinds accuse us,
the heaviness of the curtains,
and the noise tastes like a dusty market.

Dying in a hotel
at the count of three and a doubtful draw,
the heart fails, the knees unhinge from the frame,
the spoken body does not preach its true face
neither the gospel expels us from the party
of God nor from Marx.

A squad of moisture covers the sheets,
although our children refuse to be born under this haze.

Dying has its grace, its absurd sentence.
Without a week to write nor Monday to walk,
the longing for this death brings a slogan abolished
by the thigh´s night; an outdoor punishment
beneath Whitman Island.
Poe Park is a weighty memory, an avenue trapped
by its own ephemeris crawls beneath the cold.
Finger inside, one by one, one arrives, this avenue
opens its humidity, we cross a city besieged by fear;
it suffers from its stolen pens or good notebooks,
for an incense that is leaving far away from a navel,
that recovers the activated consonant nasality
because of a memory, an N or a letter that is not even a vowel
nor is it Greek when predicting sequences of screams.

Supreme cowardice does not redeem the motel
or the dead. That futile darkness invents and clarity betrays.
That dark territory does not erase the bodies off their ruin.
The caprice house is a good place to die in plural
without the landings on an elbow interrogation,
or a hair amnesia; eyelashes can think their story,
open within the fog of a few feet of withdrawn land.
From there, sex is as anonymous as the fetus born
from this sweet ant —it works its armpit and licks its slang.

There is no moral to judge this predicate
that goes silent. This subject without sentence,
the guilt is empty of morals.
Sense deflates its semantics of useless months.
Death proclaims its trophy, touches its dartboard
and rounds its abstinence in the dark of this creeping child.

This calendar must have burned hours ago.
It could have hurt before, moaned afterward;
the earthquake does not deprive its January dead.
Questions die, affirmations are established
on the other side of the sea, of good,
of this dinner of bones under smoke.

There is a virtual theater, perhaps a cinema,
to taste the pain of this infamous bliss;
it delights us with its wild grapes.
It nails its exquisite vane a few steps from its ass.
There is a centimeter of inexplicable whim,
the centimeters shall judge the strike
and the waiting for this orgasm —this bodily death
on its canvasses, free of pity
on the ankles of this burning and spiteful garlic.

A body is like a dart,
it enters without permission, on the edge
it twists the course, floats over the cement,
opens its lips; it hits the mark,
unpainting the doors, grinding the nails´ lock.

It enters the center, hits the edge, breaks with its flight.

It rushes the weak point from this shaded mass.
A bush has been born, the rose no longer speaks
about the tree nor persists in leaving lights
in the memory of these undying calories.

LOVE ON A BICYCLE
AND OTHER POEMS

(New York, 2010)

Translated by Pilar González, María Postigo,
& Carrie Summerford.

Forbidden waters

As you sleep
I cross below the bridges
that plunge yesterday or tomorrow
into despair —time of useless ferocities.

Nothing will alter the course of this haste
that juxtaposes anguish
or the river of an irrevocable beginning.

To avoid an avenue devoid of adventure,
blessed is the wandering of the water
from this haste to the reunion with the stones
of my ancestors. Or persecuted by a pilgrimage
of happy corpses. I plant my feet on the color of March.

Or on any afternoon, surrendering my body
to the words that do not flow, that never manage
the founding of your smile,
they flirt with the frivolity of your legs.
Persistence of a womb of morbid questions,
there are extremities leaning against
an antique armchair, where we could
have made the love of the month.

Lost among ghosts,
somebody steps on our heels.
Let's go, let us walk away
from this horizon
or return to this daily pain,
slobbery —like the sea of our infancy.

Your lips

They will utter two millenniums of insults,
damnations of a vertiginous day,
horizontal pride of dying without saying goodbye.

There are consonant voids, debauchery of being.
                    There are signs.
I have loved you in the uncertainty of infamy,
first words, clumsiness in conviction.

Your lips have already reunited a carnival
of wise men. A patron will die in the scaffolding
of a matchstick if it still hurts to be tepid
in the silent blindness of ardor.

Any one of these days they will return.
Regretful of a speech, they copulate in the gas chamber.
Where today they err.
If they are not inclined to die,
we are redeemed by judgement.

To find your chapped lips,
a journey towards tedium.
I feel them irreverent, latching
onto the nipples of a mountain,
returning to the confines of the navel.

Since then the firmness of pain has lips,
your body flows in the humidity of the cinnamon.
Stones do not subjugate a forest of reef.
How fertile the cry of the desert!

Oh, the burning of forgotten volcanoes!
It would make sense to separate geography
or to invent a wandering mouth.
If it is never discovered,
the urgent *Ouch* of emptiness
will never cede its dominance.

If the world has sanity,
it should reason for your promises,
answer for your hairs.
Perhaps we will consider a pack of dogs
without god or wine already senses the craving in the neck.

The city evicts the delusion of questions.

I feel your teeth gnawing at stale bread,
opening to engulf a mangrove;
they absorb the skeleton of an umbrella,
and reclaim the beginning of this orgy.

Levels of time

Bring out our daily cacti
and the confusion of your tender hands,
50 minutes of eternity to conceive the illusion
of this aurora, 33 degrees weaken this orchid,
land of martyrs, painted faces.

Why hide a mistake in the ankle?
Or a call discovered on a phone line dead of shame?

When you close curtains, goodbyes are born,
somersaults of thought,
doubts of being heard from another star.

Today no cold seeds will grow,
we shall await another uninhabited galley,
a future delirium shall renounce all doubt,
if some saints cross between the satyrs
of the desert. The morning of a pubis insists
on waking closely, stars are being vandalized
still rediscovering the agora of the wind
or untying forests seas, slow felines hidden
amid the grass of splendor.

You no longer tackle the perplexity of life,
you simply conquer a pleasure,
throw ashes into the ocean or an uncertain island
loses its horizon, a thorn promised to hope.

The farewell bleeds from its gut feeling.

Delays of the sea

I wanted to write time,
but the sea kept moving away.

It still rumbles against my ears
or its sound stops, takes its time
in bringing down the stones of the past.
One day it will gnaw at the mountains where I think of you.

This house of bones borrowed
without interest will also fall,
destroyed by your hands,
tangled by your hair —that insoluble today.

Afternoon of useless warriors,
stubbornness of feeling
—when not-feeling has unleashed the void.
Since yesterday,
tomorrow remains unpronounceable.

I see on the horizon your body in disuse.
Serious question, hazy scourge of a futureless wind.
My today should be the remnant of a non-transferable past.
A fire creates time consumed, sweet burn,
it doesn't invoke grass of hope.
An end where the efforts to save
the bodies scorched by the errant rain fail.

Ravens in the twilight

When the ravens rejected your eyes
there was a dispute against the dogs
            —insatiable of sleep.

Silence imposed heavy bars,
tears and cries returned birds to noon,
eyeglasses, flowers fleeing from a dissolved garden.

Your hands were winning
the battle of uncertainty,
sparking fireworks without heroisms,
hollowness of bells under a sordid silence,
defiance of the spring,
your glorious nails rid shadows of smoldering chants,
rising up to the knees to save a raven from the terror
hidden in a cup of coffee, howling at midnight
to release a thought:
a landscape of escapes earned us a park.

I think they stole from us
breads that refused to multiply.
We had so much music in our hands,
so many fixed stars; and airplanes
scared the trees invaded by birds of prey.

It happened when our thoughts separated mirrors.
Even then, we had gained enough nakedness or too much clarity.

Multiples of one

To love each other, we need only one heart.
Then ignorance adds another, excessive discomfort, senseless
questions, absurd aggravation of living, a back,
an eye and other round things, some ovals,
a stroll of umbrellas when it rains in the month of devouring.
We will also miss detaching ourselves from our hands.

Uh, the masses, excessive self-digging,
retaining, being content with the sigh of a slow thumb
or with the furious stay of the older brother.
Pointing at you, enough audacity, headless bodies,
at random one of the two will prevail in the disdain
or the error of evoking absence,
beautiful navel, of the anus that cuts
bitemarks loose, talking bruises.

Being intelligent, furious, arrogant
requires a certain math, or asking ourselves
how many times we have happened to ourselves
or been preceded by other bodies, organs,
musical notes, stained wood against your buttocks
that retain an innocent finger's humor
or propose a belated inflammation,
those hardships we confront,
playful rivers of sweat,
they can drown cacti
in the desert, flood lakes
or clear the dead
falling behind on the first round.

Achilles' heel

After the randomness of running into each other, we made the mistake of summoning Cervantes or expelling the Clintons from our ironies. God, whatever their identity, repressed their doubt over the cardinal points. We had opened up a lake to navigate with breadth towards a lost land or a mystery.

We made our way randomly, fashionably, house of spirits, talking up a storm, concealing the conjugal chess game, a gesture, the idea of eternity, given that they would need immigration papers, certifications, promises, Chinese ink stamps, and telephones to discover an area of intellect, or a stronghold forgotten on a back, the map of the infinite, then on to abandoning Cervantes and resorting to certain moments with Quevedo or Góngora.

An auction of it all didn't make the same sense as finding a place for it, better to take the dog out slowly and then spontaneously, put him in the yard, in the living room we used for visiting suicides, even the spoken body does not respond to the taboos of a new language, to the romanticism of the daily omissions, ruminations, pure growling; tends to behave by motorizing new contortions, to the heat of a complaint or a cry. It detaches itself from conventions. That is why the poem flirts. Limbs could consume the sea, unleash a deluge if by chance you discover heels, ankles, the suspense of ellipsis, affirmations, or decreed denials—a legal raffle.

We go towards a street filled with vanilla ice cream, fruit, falsified promenades, or a game in which we must find a spot hidden at the end of buttocks, under the nipples covered with rusty necklaces and beautiful moles, from the forehead protected by berets that change colors or stripes, depending on the time of day or on the trees.

Love on a bicycle

Torture bandages the eyes, convicted by pleasure.
The lovers provide clavicles, migraines.
They do not keep track of time.
The cat-like night unearths an orphanage,
incriminates the other face of emptiness.

Pins fall daily over its clarity,
smoke bombs, incense.

A bicycle circles the afternoon in search of love.

Doors were lost, the sun stays too long, notebooks last moons,
more stars return to summon the leap, the journey of hiding
ourselves caresses a broken compass. The determination
to self-destruct instates torture, illuminates its chains,
a surge of deaf bonfires brings back a naked dog
and the morning loosens up canes in order to walk around,
circling through blind corridors,
children who border an unbreathable river.

In the middle of reason, someone dynamites silence.

It disappears devouring a piano,
surrounded by an absurd freedom
and that battle with light that makes them ragged, rabidly useless.

Today they lost their feet. Later on,
love will consume their liver,
then it will chew the remains of a laughable lung,
but they will not intimidate the distant beams
of an unfortunate bicycle that has lost its way.

THE KINGDOM
OF THINGS

(New York, 2011-2012)

Translated by Juanita Eslava Bejarano.

The beautiful nothing

The beautiful nothing
leaves its servitude cold,
devours flowerpots, dirty green leaves;
and cacti roll leaving controls in the gutter.
There are tracks that predict a perfume.
Tired heels scatter a verb.
There is an excess of repressed pain at the doors.
This garden fights its last battle.
The contradiction happens, fear worms in,
grinding pokes its glorious thongs;
especially now the salt prevents rereading
the food-smasher of cracks,
a dark waist expels sensuality
that tastes of pork rinds
and it pops into my head
to smell the pallor of this selflessness.

The lemon has lent its white peel.
Its lack of seed lies. This green flatters,
vinegars its nakedness.
Obtuse, the triangle of glasses laughs.
There is no lunatic rice
moaning between the sheets of this story.

There is an undergrowth of begging objects.
This absurd poem is redeemed from you
and melancholy frees its shadows.
The absurd wind no longer brings the sea,
just a deluge of ridiculous and rough things.

The empire of things persists,
gnawing at us, devouring nights,
writing a tragedy
between the edges of the tablecloth.

There is an oil that refuses to define the low flame,
a castrated countryside,

the whole walks wearing the city as a uniform.
It curls up indifferently among old cheeses
and the iodine opens its gauze.
The wounds opened their cigar butts,
they injected defeated cities.
There is the humor of this absent landscape,
                                    ships and dead.

There is a garden covered in imported blouses.

Without crayons there is no romance,
but the chopsticks sweat,
by opening, the meats vegetate.
God's infantry groups together,
these soldiers of hungry
turpentine lick their honey.

The mustard persists,
the red devil spits gall over the stove.
There are lips holding back its thoughts.

There is a laughing friendship
between the ketchup and the brown sugar;
luck touches the warm lips
of the one bound to live for another hour.

The lust of this twilight stops frowning.
The glorious one leaves its goring,
nails a bull between the cliffs.
But luck caresses the balls of this lost eye.
The twin controls taste their salt, bite their abyss;
the cards hurt without dying.
They do not write even the I's of Vaseline.
The poem wields the guilt
and its objections taste their ashes.

The radio no longer thinks,
the penknife pokes eyes out
with its green numbers.
And there are black stripes

no one will read. A chipped nail tip.
The book has muted its pen.
The pencil complains about this nonsense,
sacred cow segregation and smug horns.

The cry has gone silent.
The notes devoid of songs gravitate
over the potassium.
But if you raise the cattle, free the paper
                    —stormy rain affair.
There is a childish barbecue, but you can fast now
and it's time to run without *quinielas*,
                without postage stamps.

There is constancy of the number and steps,
roar of lions and larvae. Ending a dispute
with the goblins of a contradiction,
the complaint on things no longer hides
its verbs. Their empty plates bleed butter
sad stalactites. There are burial mounds,
desperate reefs burning.

The rumor does not deprive us
of more imbeciles. Depraved time reigns.

The hours flee from their greasy niche,
predict utensils to deposit authority,
and treacherous vessels vacate another era.

The refrigerators curl up with laughter,
hollow melodies, dead radios, desolate televisions.

Without contemplation nothingness arrives.

There is a city of warnings, of grim receipts,
fading torsos, shady company.
The photographs warn about can openers:
we have discovered a nude in the greedy can openers,
a map to burp on a clumsy lighter.

There are tender slogans
and round-eyed logos roll;
bedrooms sleep in the chimneys,
ruminate their ash burst.
The realest life rushes vitamins
in the cliffs of this pain,
the crying sews lost children on
the outskirts of this mountain.
The poet chews gums,
hoards lipstick and spits out sawdust.

The vitamins no longer let me see the car.
These genocides close their windows.
And the day furnishes its amazement
under the captive grass.
There is a tree rotting with love.
At the bottom of this bliss there are eggshells
and kisses that fade in the *quinielas* of this deluge.

There is a town on the other side of the world,
empty on the other side of I; nothing inhabits
the poem of the symbols tired of being rushed,

but there are specters of used cinnamon.
Sweet cloves scratch the tea,
announce an empty city romance.

Worth suffering,
it is still possible to open the hands
and deny sensuality. The finger goes cold
to discover a useless and arrogant heat,
a farewell whim.
Sink your fangs of peace,
hasten your backteeth;
the romance of things has imposed its law.

It doesn't happen,
but I get tired of this calyx and this dull wine.
I'm tired of the latrines of this cinema,
of this brown sugar passion.

I am Frida after the accident,
a Byron who returns,
a Lautréamont's infamy
of these cheeses without a prison story,
of this fog without smoke.

I am a written name in the emptiness
of a clean hospital.
I do not tire of being a tiger and a man,
a woman and a bird.

Neither am I the furious dart
nor the still blood of the sea.

It happens that I am not the foreigner
or a black skeptical of being the (white?)
target of the miracle stones.

On the lapidary torsos
there is some sort of absent bullet.
I am an *I*, an *I-don't-know-what*,
carrying the *you* or a pregnant reverse version.
They saw this pronoun in the corner,
the others dropped their cigar butts on time
and they went to the movies to urinate;
they gave birth to a suffix, devouring red grapes.
I never stopped pruning my cactus,
but if the verb condemns me,
I free insects, I release my fevers,
my armpit stench enjoys hallucinations.

I close the doors, slam the defeated bolts
and curse a tender child.
If infamy does not exist, neither does man,
the woman with the tree of worms.
I lock myself up to smoke my doors,
my windows and my fifteen hours
of humanitarian work;
they set me free to pace
my room on my knees, smell my urine,

trip over a smelly tin soldier,
trample over the silence of the things
that no longer preach a hecatomb
of cutlery on the desert of this street.

I am the enemy of reason,
an unfortunate of its doubts.
I was the most faithful hour
and the minute of this well-being.

Today, I feel like saying goodbye
and I must ambush my words,
The maybes gnaw, a yes flows,
this rhythm curses what's
superfluous, unscrews poses.

The deluge departs without you.
I grope my freeway day,
my abundance of lightning laughs.
Scarce of its light, the chains of this tree burst.
I go out in search of myself
and the pain makes a party in the gums.

These seductions dominate me.
The greed to go out of my way.
I don't jump off a bridge
—there are female Italian tourists.

It rains when we trace the light.
The moon is curious.
Between the black pantyhose,
they shoot hustle yolks; wires sound.
It is better to sleep on a wire and cross the avenue.
Hold a body without saliva,
an ear that gets goosebumps from hearing itself,
hoard perfumed towns,
open eyes without a piggy bank,
melt lips if the dogs of this

confinement do not bark,
denounce an orchid, effeminate a ball,
release the fence of its most genuine legs,
of its filial bridges and pervert
for an hour these claims.

The rain flutters its priesthood
and inexplicably caresses this shadow.

SONG FOR THE CITY THAT INHABITS US

(New York, 2012)

Translated by Juanita Eslava Bejarano.

If nails gallop over the bleeding back

If nails gallop over the bleeding back while we run on the steed of this orgy, a pious city conceives us, gives birth to us on the sidewalk, breaks alcohol fountains to wash the blinds of this morning in the workshops, wages dog fights, and leaves us dragging a cage, an empty fishbowl, a furious orchid at the time of goodbye. Novelized without throwing a strike, it moves the televisions and unhooks its mortuary boxes to inhabit a street. So much it falls apart when touched, it dreams of falling apart. It screams from the non-place. It howls like a bilingual cockroach, free and sovereign. It claims to be a city and takes us in the train of fraternal silences, in the runaway lemon, in the castrated limes. I kiss its soft hooves, slabs entrenched in the dream. The *montra* gravels its cold coins on the remains of the antifreeze; it throws sludge to chase away winged rats. It ruminates and runs to arrive on time to the Jamaica Center of the rolling sternum. It remains ready to illuminate a deaf word. The blind snake enters the viewpoint of the repealed courtyards by this invasion of clean flies; its transparent ballast shakes a sad puberty. Loads and scraps were needed to finish the week of the seven condemned to the clock, ready to carry up to thirty the hopes of this orgasm.

If the city read Machado

If the city read Machado or lied naked dialoguing with Baudelaire, extinguishing the chandeliers, biting pears and scratching the wall empty of questions that have no answer, perhaps the absent kids would come. No city suffers from more glorious whoredoms nor more august vile actions, only from deaf genitals and cones said aloud, If I put flowers on the birds' table, more wings and fewer breasts would come to die, more rum and radios turned off forever. There would be a night ready to unleash the darts that never hit the breasts of the city; neither would the navel pity those who ask for an orgy, nor the legs burn under the keys of a room without an eye because of desire. The cries of the melancholy of a brave finger would increase, crows would come to frighten the sleep in the armchair, for so much hell there is no need of river or cheeses that take revenge of waiting for the holy game.

Within all the visited cities

Within all the visited cities, there is one willing to bury the notebooks with academic rush and without mystery. No need for *bachata* in the *batey*, *merengue* at the wake or a *reggeaton* born in haste in a lapidary cellar and much less a Tina Turner concert or an anecdote of summer thieves cooling off in another city or corpses wandering back to Amsterdam or smiling from a morgue in the Aztec district. I might do it (it's even probable): drowning a stolen pen without meaning to, forgiving the joke and regretting the civilized gesture, but there they only read perfumed suicides like Gianni Versace, with broken alligators on the shore of this lake, but pawnbrokers also read for the zeal of their accounts, parrots read. They vomit a rosary for those who still have eyes to read a will, hands to weigh the thread paper and caress a borrowed letter without any interest.

ALKA-SELTZER

(New York, 2013)

*Translated by Alyssa King, Pilar González, María Postigo,
& Carrie Summerford.*

Who will defend us for loving Martin Luther King?

Who will save us
from returning to the deposit of fresh bones?
—to squeeze the oranges from the fantasy tree—
we should have raised our hands
and run beyond the drunken graves,
stunned by those little twilight cars,
filled with unbearable progress
where have they dismantled the tenderness
in the pockets of the miserable.

If there is news yet, who will protect us
from those who still look for Narcissus?
Where are the Tablets of the Law of the judges
that work arduously to condemn our shadows?
Of the police that don't sleep searching
between the verbs needed to conjugate
the happiest trigger in the world?

—even if the tenderness of those
who loved us too much is better.

Who am I to invoke severed pencils

Who am I to invoke severed pencils
and the permanent ink of those who flee
to another bare shelf, guarded
by the most romantic elite in the world?

They have come to get what's theirs
and left in pursuit of the antipoetic ghosts
of the great poetry written in beauty salons,
deciphered in the landfills of the sentimental
Malecón of smiling despair.
There we sharpened the most presidential pencil in the world.

Who will defend us from the authoritarian pronouns,
from the inexplicable 'usted'
and the buried proximity of gardens?
Or from the accomplice 'us'?
Always ready for the promiscuous daytime hotel date.

Who will say: here is the public defender
against oppression lowered out of the haze,
twilight, when terror divides the city and feeds on Edward
Snowden's pencils, chase the haunting rhetoric of Julián Assange?

Do you just tight-rope over the equator of secrets?

Who promises classics
for the boredom of good taste?

Who promises traditional boas perfumed with madness,
suicides sleeping religiously in the hygienic act of kissing
the orgasmic face of God, the wolf's ferocity
that no longer holds the presidential band of modesty?

Do victims howl from the mountains of pain,
without questioning the landscape?

Who will defend the imperialist intoxication
of the great worldly paradise,
of the animals lined up at the hour
of the signing of the death
of a country, if there is a judgment hour
for those who defecate on the flowers
of a stubborn city in its doom?

Who will defend us from a company of cunning pickpockets,
from biblical oaths, and from a council under
the uncertain drums of the absence of so many apostles
willing to sell their balls for a hazy walkway?
Of imprisoned vaginas, gray nipples
of an empire without barbers?

Either they existed or belched from a dissenting thought,
an empty question or a pink dysentery.

Did they not go from the hand of imperialism focused
on the most diverse loneliness of the Nobel Peace Prize
 or the multiplication of the brutes of feeling?

Why does this comedy without Interest tax reek so badly?

Who will defend us from allowing the invasion
of this smell into the bedrooms of those who
still think of their comfortable solitude?

Who will converse with the utopic,
heartless socialism that won't let the imaginary
marketing network to live eternally?

Is there love more virtual than losing
the motherland and not asking the brain
if it has a mouth to belch on the saliva
of empty bottles of an unfaithful caravan?
Or if the limbs carry a nice scent after an underarm exam?

What a disgrace that I will not be the last minority of silence!
What divine and dull clumsiness that I have not been
the target of official charities, deprived of their backside
or the singular stuntman of this militancy in the fall!

Does the path to independence suffer
from inappropriate bleach agents
or is its proclamation tasteless?

What blandness migrates from all pasts to destroy
a deficit laugh of the future? Which imperialism
sickens the independence of this fragmented island,
of this sea that bathes the distance with queries?

Or does it have to flee
to think of the misfortune of glamour?

Why do I threaten to descend
toward my own shadow?

What Messiah do I suffer from?

No one can cure this Sacerdotal delirium
nor bury a cheerful Mahoma
on the denounced horizon.

Yorubas and Mandelas of the great
African south arrive. We march anew
to the past in search of a black Lone Ranger
who has never been to Harlem.

For suspicion, there is the much-needed
George Washington; there is a bridge filled
with frozen turkeys, very far from the *never ever*,
from the starched *perhaps* or the dismal *yes*
of a Labor Day Parade; the profits are not divided
into little pieces tied with bat wings.

Will there ever come a foolishly hopeful *may*
or tax caresses of the universal narcocracy?

Why do I give myself the luxury
of dying so far and living so near?

Who will protect us from the racialized
industriousness of usurping intelligence?

The colonized only obey superior orders.
The empty stomach's ecclesiastical spring asks
the aristocrat for order; the wise intelligence
disintegrates into a smile.

In the past caress of the silenced butterflies
awaits a garden devoured by love,
vain for burning in its wax.

Mercenary world, for the suspicious punctuality
of the deaf and the cleanliness of the walls.
Gasoline arrives on time to the streets
and the lights expose its heroism,
even thoughthe mirror of anguish is needed.

Is there democracy in being on one's knees
reading the psalm of the condemned?

Who will protect us from so much universal glory,
from so much work in favor of a tourism in ruins?

Set aside, deaf world, the blindness that prevents
you from noticing the adulterous angels' goblet.

Tell me once more
who will protect us from a convict?

Accused, vilified prisoner, condemned to his
embassy. Who will let him enter between those
infinite meters of freedom if they still call him Julian Assange?

Who will protect us from those that lock up a bird
in a still ship's kitchen if it still flies among
the dead encaged by illusion?

Tell me now, officer, devil's advocate,
happy contractor, civil soldier, wind agent,
death legislator, why has the condemned
not ceased to be Edward Snowden
if he still flies between the bars
of demolished statues?

A new journalism has emerged from the decay.

If love makes it to this week's agenda

Where is the day's hook?

I threw the harpoon
and caught the eye of a suicide victim,
the hand of a poet lost in paradise.

If my house is your haven, hide.

My arms are the path,
but you must be the destination
of that scattered route where everything ends.

The trees no longer perfume the morning of freedom.
The wretched, we only have the joy of writing eulogies from
Jamaica Center or the Brooklyn Bridge imagined in the Bronx.

The letters have disappeared from the secret agendas
of the colonized. There are baroque diarrhea and letters
waiting for a recipient.
The enigma was discovered:
the empty tables in the academic
shantytown's harbor are no longer waterborne.

The first night of love paints its back ruined
by the nails of María Auxiliadora.

The memory of a salty tongue suffers from its
misfortune, a sweetness that meditates on a beach
as remote as the origin of the wind though
the horizon is the limit of the last flowers.

DISPOSABLE GOSPEL

(New York, 2016)

Translated by Alyssa King.

Dew of awakening

And to you, anonymous being made of mundane words, for
dedicating to me the hands of dawn, that feeling of sovereign
bones and sign of a sky that still holds the cloak of a steadily
tender star. It's a sovereign and sweet
dawn to walk upon the dew of black herbs
that cannot question the feet
if they do not know the embarrassing
and absurd route of the stairs that await.
The dough waits for a coffee promised
to the tracks. My heart cannot walk to your body
but it can still hear bells when your words
undermine the silence
and curse it at the foot of a cross.

1 Corinthians 12:21-22

In the sensual dialogue of the senses,
eyes are born for the saying's offering
and there are pages held by a blind hand.
I flaunt the eyes of her skin when the refusal
of pleasure requires shadows.
Touch doesn't have a head
either for meditating feet.
At the hour of desire,
The feet drift over the first sacrifice's chest.
The mouth prays about the hardness of the cross. The Father of
all languages translates a compass's virtue when the ships arrive.
He says, "I do not need you
but I am the refuge for the members of a body.
I award the weakest with flames that burn with textual wisdom."

A poem for Berta Cáceres

I was thoroughly fascinated by what
the fisherman of Galilee said:
'I can no longer walk upon the waters
or humiliate the fishermen of sand.'
In Flint, Michigan, the fish did not multiply either. Environmental
terrorism awaits
with March's last surprise:
Berta Cáceres didn't lose sensuality
with her unexpected departure
to a Mayan kingdom and beyond.
The romance of beeless flowers returns
to shake the streets of Honduras
in this painful March of 2016.
Now I believe that we must turn off the lights
but first accuse of ingratitude those who
lower the flag and let humanity rest from
the tediousness of national anthems.
Colonial archeology still jumps over
the meek horses of the new
border of Hispanophilia.

Electronic passion

It's just that when I let myself be seduced
by the original sin of electronic exile,
the Lord comes and convinces me to return
to the irrational paradise of heat,
and I obey His eternal patrimonial orders.
He, who knows it all, without having
heard of the latest technological revolution,
comes to my bed and drags me into
a tropical bubble. He takes a photo of me.
We don't go on Facebook. He makes a video of my suffering, but
doesn't share it—not even with Judas. He takes me by surprise.
I feel Him breathe inside of me.
He, a polyglot, dominates all axioms
concerning feeling and emotion.
He revises my debts and helps me put in order
the lack of credit in the geometrical gaze.
After, He deciphers the adoration of my tears. Then his great
smell allows me to enter
His chambers naked, but He doesn't
look at me with malice, like the narrator
of this story. He just takes my hands and allows me to sit at His
feet in order to help me to purge
my longings for survival; and, since I am
another male Magdalena, I decide to lay my head on His knees to
be forgiven for all of the sins
I have not been able to commit.
Then, the Creator runs His hands over the back
of my neck, so that I will feel that I am not alone and will not
resist.
Thus, I surrender to His memory.

1 Corinthians 1:27-29

And it wasn't true that God chose the fool
of the world to tidy up paradise.
He did not think about how weak I am
to claim surprise to the gullible
with an hour of physical wisdom.
I have not been able to achieve the joy of fearing
his absence. I didn't even worship His crucified historical Grace. I
have not recognized
the purgatory of His more intimate testamentary genealogy. I
haven't been shown
the face of my beloved nor the smell
of the flowers that escaped from paradise
to humiliate the environmentalists;
and the weak of the world chose the one
who sees from the eyes of an iguana,
to surprise suspicions in the hands
that left a body exiled between bubbles
of hard skin that do not ignore their love of sin.
To shame the strong,
I erred toward an imaginary pain;
and the vile of the world tended to useless jealousies and the
despised chose the one who
knows too much about the failures of the world,
in order to confuse the pride in fear's skin,
and it was the joy of loose hair and the surprise
of a piano that doesn't give away so much curious
sensuality beneath international waters.
It only shows an intelligent clamor,
without memory or fear of hope to undo
that which is, so that no one boasts in his
presence of having possessed its shadow.

Disposable Gospel

I am fortunate to hear
the absence of an "I love you"
when there is no direction in fate.
Doubt's pretentious fertility woos
a notion of imperfect hooks.
They discriminate if your mouth sabotages
the seas, or if your body floats in order to rescue the failed hour
when the guitars think
about greeting noon, defying those who
hope to cross a toy bridge, to then keep it
in the smallest pocket of this bankrupt day.

SLEEPWALKING CEMETERY

(Santo Domingo, RD, 2016)

Translated by Alyssa King.

Part One:

Sleepwalking cemetery

I

If you truly want to expose yourself
to the existential danger of this recent today
or be hunted like an endangered migratory bird,
you just have to work to the point of exhaustion,
jump over these international corridors,
raising the flag of progress. In order to deceive yourself,
take serious precautions against oblivion.
Explore the remaining turbulence.

5

I am going to renounce being seen as the one
who flees toward intransitive conjugations.
I have my suspicions about quantitative adverbs.
So many aggressive mythologies must be shaken off.
The myth of God is no longer a deficit enigma.
We've stopped speaking about our misery with authority.
This outcry is a silent orgy.

10

The literature of duty flees from concave mirrors of noon.
There is always a driving force that disarms the fantasy
slaves of a night of laborious teeth.
The swords of Postmodernism inaugurate new migrations
toward the prehistory of this sleepwalking cemetery.

15

We were looking for a prize to stupidize our
longings or to play the lip-biting suicide victim
in a room where books sleep while
the most dangerous bohemian in the world stays up late.

20

Reading a poem is more dangerous
than hearing the seller of whimsical metals walk
on sand to hear how nothingness defies the senses.
The sea offers fewer dangers than eating
pan de fruta at the end of a poem once again.

25

If I go any which day toward another coldness
it should be because all seasons here have been exhausted.
The summer is as irreconcilable
as the fraud of a decapitalized wall.
Meaning is the triumph of meaninglessness.
I set off from an island that is no longer surrounded by ghosts.
It has been interrogated by misery and takes refuge
under the silence of a poem like a monthly
paycheck discredited by the utopia of reason.

30

It makes no sense to take revenge on those who leave.
Or question their return. Nor to shoot down
the one who left in search of a less dreary deportation.
They are afraid of abandonment.
Among these brave ones, there are those who
claimed a damp street or a rebellious skirt.

They heroically defended their flags.
They protected a colonial shield, unknowingly.
They were as Rosicrucian as the Trinitarians
of 1844. Others painted walls with images
of the fallen or dug a tunnel to get home.

35

If dying is fun, write a deficit testament.
Do not allow the gravediggers to perform
tricks with a sweet femur,
a still undead index can be a sign.
Check the pulse of the eye surprised
of being alive. Start paying in advance
for your digital footprints.
If a leaf ascends, we question the roots
Of another amnesty.
Force them to military services
while they look at you, while they smell
your rags or curse the lack of wood
at rest time or the nakedness of the lucid body
that can only be described
as a season of reconciliation.

40

Each time I get up, I'm startled by the treachery
of the skeletons that invade the house,
ignoring that there are others that don't know
the confinement of a robe.
An orgy of incomprehensible mutations commences.

They don't question the shallowness
of those who don't sleep embracing
the sweet basin of a viewpoint full of bells.

47

Imminent Notice:
Priest lost among the secrets of a veiled burial
that is a luxury of the State.
The Viacrucis has fled the apathy of the walls
and the empty niche is the house of the future.
Here, only the dead looks at their bone cage
to discover the cause of oblivion.
A statement is required to nationalize
the suffering of those who left for a suspicious destiny.

Part two:

Poetic exhumation

I am sad

I presumed that I was different from you all.
I wanted to lie in the same way and be gloomy
and petulant, but I lacked the strength for so
much corporate imagination. I am fed by a
fertile idleness of some underground ghetto.

You all are not to blame completely for my happiness.
I fall belatedly into an atrocious consciousness.
I asked you to give what I could not.
We could celebrate my existential
failure and your success in collecting bills
from others or fattening up on this
                    metaphysical boredom.
You have been bolder in making sense
of what I refused to accept as the destiny
of being. I am no longer overwhelmed
by those firm and fierce steps toward
a useless freedom to describe in a poem.

There is a libertarian vacuum among
the delinquents surprised by an intolerable
wisdom, good for scaring the clumsy.
I was impoverished by the ethics of duty,
the suspicious morality of the statues
that pigeons shit on, and you were
enriched by accounting for sweet hypocrisy.

I sensed the beauty of a creeping, applaudable
gesture. It keeps the world's ashes standing
and the revenge of being as an indulgent heroism.

159

Where is my hope if I am addicted
to the beautiful idiocy of being happy.

The hope you drag along the reefs of these gloomy seas.
You laugh at uncertainty and struggle
to make my footsteps trip. Trains do not help me escape.

The cannibals of spirit flee upon noticing such
                        —consecration to innocence.

To help those condemned to sleeplessness

To buy an automatic eyeopener
or hire a seductive robot that threatens
the lucidity of smokers with a seductive perfume.
They don't dream or have hope.
They aren't bisexual or heterosexual.
They have no kids or write on purgatory's tombstones
but, in regard to sleep, I have suggested that we help
sleepwalkers for safety reasons
and others for the vanity of pajamas.
They can confuse doors;
fire escapes can delay the arrival of blood,
the wait for urine; and they can postpone agony's fecal matter.
You have to distribute sleep equally,
but in the meantime, set up hospital beds in the closets,
bring discreet roosters, trumpets with Tonsillitis,
or donate slippers so that they can read the reactants
during the transition from one dream to another
or read the chemical composition of dismay,
work for them until the centrifuge makes it predictions of death.

I see musical notes on the left arm of a traveler

A signature on the muscle of the right arm.
Someone else's wall watches fish
in someone's hands.
Daily memory is a long, inhuman wall,
a neck painted with a kiss, an ear drawn
on an elbow's shadow, a mobile niche.
Absent flowers shine on the sway of the train
that takes our bones toward the odd-numbered
path where the drawn tone is no longer
in the wrong names. Beings return on foot,
empty shoulders jump silently,
monotonous hands sleep free of schemes
—they play a song that distinguishes
their nakedness in the awakening
where someone else carries their stars
on their arm or hides dangerous moons
in their chest or hints of a heavenly body when it shows up.

DAKA DAKA DAKA, DREAMERS AND THE TRAIN OF THE DEAD

(New York, 2017)

Translated by María Postigo & Erin Mangan.

DAKA DAKA DAKA

Daka Daka, Daka
Daka Daka, Daka
Daka Daka, Daka
Trust this love, be trustful, Daka
Come, chase your dream
and defend this house, Daka
My love, if you fight, we will win, Daka
Daka Daka, Daka
Daka Daka, Daka
Daka Daka, Daka
Without true justice the cow will die, Daka
Oh Daka, official justice is not poetic, Daka
Oh Daka, I have stones in my throat, Daka
Oh Daka, the ocean is knocking on my door, Daka
Oh Daka, my ankles are chained, Daka
Daka Daka, Daka
Daka Daka, Daka
Daka Daka, Daka
If the white river is already inside the house, Daka

What should we do with this genocide, Daka
If they have a knife to my throat, Daka
I must be with you to push fear away, Daka
Daka Daka, Daka
Daka Daka, Daka
Daka Daka, Daka
Flags always pass, Daka
There is no peace but chimeras, Daka
I'm here to surprise you, Daka
A free star awaits us, Daka
Daka Daka, Daka
Daka Daka, Daka

Daka Daka, Daka

Oh Daka, why in injustice so powerful?
Jail has become a storm, Daka

Out of misery grow the bars, Daka
Daka Daka, Daka
Daka Daka, Daka
Daka Daka, Daka
Who snatches my hope, Daka?
Where is my mom hiding, Daka?

Where do I find my dad, Daka?
Daka Daka, Daka
Daka Daka, Daka
Daka Daka, Daka
Where are our papers buried, Daka?
Tell me who controls hope, Daka
Tell me now, this is my house, Daka
Daka Daka, Daka
Daka Daka, Daka
Daka Daka, Daka
Oh Daka, I'm no longer a simple stake, Daka
Hurry, the pain is overpowering, Daka
Oh Daka, I distrust every wall, Daka
Daka Daka, Daka
Daka Daka, Daka
Daka Daka, Daka
If this life was destined for love, Daka
I live the freedom of being fire, Daka
Let the blissful words fly, Daka
Daka Daka, Daka
Daka Daka, Daka
Daka Daka, Daka
Trustingly, come with me to the march, Daka

Without your loyalty I have no hope, Daka
If we fight together, little will be a lot, Daka

Daka Daka, Daka
Daka Daka, Daka
Daka Daka, DACA

The train of the dead

In order to amuse the dead
the train draws a city on the two backgrounds
The one that left me to ride down
on 7th Avenue painted quilts
for those that had died in a mortgaged winter.
The other one brings the homesickness
of the station where the bodies
become charitable deeds.
The arteries grow.
There are veins where we kiss the wound.
There is a poem that dies in the chests
but the sweet crows fly by;
they peck mommies' sensual broach
because the wave of heat consumed
the belly button. We died in the beaches
and in the parks or about the furniture
of a funeral-like hotel where my daughter
had various experiences with the dead
and with the music
(another form of death—with a musical note
trapped in the throat)
Or a guitar that was the war or the false peace.
We don't arrive in Egypt on time
nor to the photography cartridges of birthdays
Your first photo album—buried in the dead
sea of the Bronx—
Then the photographer disappeared.

A hungry gigolo arrived with two dead girls
and a absent mother—who also took care
of two dead children. I suspected once more
that she might be my daughter.

The final day of the graduation of *dreamers*
those *dreamers* that return to the cemetery
of a useless school. The students already lost
the confidence in civilized life.

167

The teachers' only vocation is dying.
We don't know anything about the feeling
of this conspiracy nor where the Daka
of an agreement with indifferent white lilies may be hiding.

THE LIMITLESS ISLAND OF LOLLIPOPS

(New York, 2018)

Translated by Erin Mangan & Guillermo Contreras.

The Odyssey of lollipops

To the great worldwide poetry of dry land

The sea woke him up gracefully
with another crisis of silly heresy.
The man of aerial justice does not know if
the awakening palettes have an imminent
destination of saliva. The refugee walks
around in tears, his pneumonia groans
upon noticing of a window judgment,
he intends to decipher the mysterious
                —skin of the wind.
There is a portentous tide over the garbage
of the wave breaker. The wind tosses
multicolored sand. There are winged
crustaceans grasping uselessly
to the desire for a wet window.
The foam of horror hits.
A newborn hurls the udders of alcoholic
cows to torment a senseless patriot.

My sternum discovers wet masks on silt
scented with aquatic tenderness.
Warning for the masked men of
independence: they draw on their sober
boats to the hairy shore
in an open triangle of interrogation.
There is a compass of hope
reviving a kiss in the shadow.
I see the deaf argument of the lone ball.
The ground keeps brushing against
the blue smoke of an inconsistent rain.
The caress of a torrential sigh still floats.
A drowned reef continues to look for you.
It knocks on the doors of the forgotten city.
An anonymous caress should
arrive on the first perforated lifesaver

171

of a femur without a compass.
Its black color is used to painting homes on
silence. A disoriented eagle poses hungrily
around the mouth of this ridiculous
purgatory. A rented tire paralyzes
the dunes of this questionable desert.
There is the sea, undercapitalized
mermaids bid their farewell.
Present me the floss of this subversive
background.

Bittersweet sigh of merciful sand.

By surprising
the sidewalks, we are assaulted by round
plantain-smashers that promote
the luxury of a false peace.
They travel from mouth
to mouth, without any
modesty or sentiment,
by the bay of a twilighting clitoris.
The ships stranded on the breeze lose their
flags. Rumor never wakes up an island full
of lollipops. They revive with a flash
of stuck between the legs.
They float on the motionless rain
of foam indifferent to their fate.

Fishing for lollipops

Staring at the sea, memories of a sad childhood come to me. Drunken men walk into the waves as I see empty bottles on the coast. The treacherous sea brings with it wet cigarette butts and used lipsticks. Rusty and cold Coca-Cola bottles float; I begin to wonder about my childhood as the compass of hopelessness is nowhere to be found. I land on an isolated island surrounded by pylons and trash. I cannot remove those flashbacks from my mind. It is with sorrow that I look back into the past. When I walked on the beach, I wore shorts, and unearthed crab bones. I just think of old glories; solemn questions about their value arise. You can see it is all a lie— the unavoidable fate of these *lollipops* floats along with the garbage of this treacherous sea. This fate brings a flood of fake promises, and then, all you see is free memories floating away in the ocean...

The indivisible island

When I land on the indivisible island, an island impossible to break into pieces, I set foot, forgetting to open my hands to measure the land. I start speaking of how great the land is from the forbidden fruits only found in cemeteries or wet crematoria where you can hear a soul crying out in pain, or a satrap raging or a hero, victim of his own misfortune, laughing. No one places raincoats on the ruins or forbids making your way through the ancient streets—flooded to save statues that perpetuate deception. You're not smelling the seaweed from the dump where crazy people love each other. We only have a few cliffs, as high as a turtle, to measure the extent of bliss. Drag your furious joy into a disposable niche.

Smart pavilions

This is the rain of another Social Friday. No one knows why we complete this quorum and add up our shadows just to gladden our enemy. There is not a single person that decides to stay home without taking the two-line subway—that clean worm that militarizes order. Our demeanor is that of an innocent baby or a stockbroker running back and forth to find a seat in the middle of that chaos. A single button represents our enter and exit. We haven't started reading or sleeping on this moving shelter. No one has come up with the idea of hiding in these cave-like coaches. Modernity is an unnoticed terrorist's best friend. I cannot hear the rain on this Friday. To ignore the garbling speech inside this circus, we pretend to be cleaning our trendy sneakers and ripping our pants while reading the horoscope. The rain shows how bad umbrellas have cheapened. The subway runs right in front of the pavilions of Paraguay, a country invited to the book fair of the Athens of the New World. You have to clean the droppings left by pigeons to cover up the imperfections of this city full of beautiful memories.

Let the chest archipelago float

Sick woman, stay in that ambiguous Emergency Room. You can't tell if you are resurrected in a Psychiatric ward. Muffle the sounds of this island storm. I can feel the very hardness of life. I glance at the sea and the breeze brings the sticky saliva of a naughty octopus and, when you say goodbye, you come to realize some kisses are deadly, and excessive praise cannot hide the desire to cry. Call the doctors. My legs hurt, the brackish and deceiving rain cannot awaken any muscles in me, yet your hymen looks like a rainbow, there is enough rain and time to count all the islands around us. Let the archipelago of your chest float, keep swimming with the organs numbed by this water, breathe the iodine of digital agony. I suffer from those cliffs that do not deny the ruins. The only thing left is the oldest streets in The Americas where a *shelter* imprisons love.

The lollipops of May

After that kiss,
may you have something greater
than a *good morning*
or an endless *see you tomorrow,*
something greater than a *maybe;*
or an *I love you* stronger than the rain
that triggers the germination
of this plant called freedom
or the growth of a sweet insult
to contradict the feeling of waiting.
I'll stop pleasing you just to perish of illusion.
Forgetting myself is indifferent to me
Just like dying with a glass of wine in my hand
ready to photograph a rose or an empty cathedral.

To preserve my sanity,
I move on to the next chapter of my memory book.

Why isn't there ever at the end of an utterance
a comma that no longer announces breaks?
Why are we talking about mom's silence
when her voice has been muted another year
                        —for the last 100 years?
One day no longer represents a pause.
Today is no longer of any value when it's nothing
but a collection of yesteryears.
It's just islands full of empty *lollipops,* sweet pieces
that shall not be part of my memory book.

Let's ignore all the rules and put an end
to the idea of vehemently believing we'll find
the right words to make others stay what word
will bring you back to reality a reality
where dreaming on is nothing but a void waste of time?

Do we have to take ourselves reach the ruins?

And climb the steps of otherness under
a proclamation of suffocating joy If love marches
against the store days and consumes altars.

I love the backroom days that spiritualize
the cassava and harden the sesame.

My muse writes, I meditate on the journey towards the gardens
of a sweet cemetery where we make love to honor the bang
of those planes that will remain flying so high above.

THE WICKED CLOWN
POEMS FOR AN ANTI-WAR IMAGINATION

(New York, 2018)

Translated by Erin Mangan, María Postigo, & Luke Johnson.

The grand march for our lives

In honor of March for Our Lives, March of 2018

Sad pencils already arrive dragging on a cadaver
while your notebooks bleed, school,
the snow screams the horror of this homicide.
Then books leap thirsty for a wasteful offering.

On the grass a dead child waits.
In the distance
lit candles and closed fists.

Bear, Parkland, this spineless humor
Invaded schools fall to their knees,
lapidary operating rooms demolished by bombs,
hospitals of a toy war,
consumed by the kings of oil
the mundane vices give birth to a filthy robot,
I feel a rumor of mathematical formulas
useful only to destroy a garden
or shut down a window
unsatisfied, the map of an unsustainable geography weeps.

Oh, Syria, where will we study the following truth
the remains of another disposable uncertainty!
The education of pleasure greets the ordinary bed
of an insufferable orgasm
I still keep hope in an asylum free of misfortune,
their desperation cannot contain me,
the ambiguous grave of sick ethics flourishes.

A tourism of sand pyramids bleeds deliriously.

Utopia plays a game of cybernetic monopoly.

There is a remote pain.

the clowns and the apostles still do not care.
lonely books in single file march in a hurry
to save the children of insensible anger.

In Yemen no one can challenge
the right to the monopoly of horror
in front of a garden of bones.
The will of the prophet
Ridicules the barbarism of this Armageddon
the collective joy of the empire
makes the poem ineffective.
Only Parkland hurts.

We are able to rewrite the ontological spelling
of this civilization immune to the truth.
Ruined signs contaminate
the gardens of paradise.

I don't know how to deny these official Christs.
The crusade risks its best preventive perfume,
not even the capital of horror is moved.
Other tyrants return to shake the memory
of this saltpeter purgatory.
The temple of Washington is extremely far
from the pious bewilderment
of the grand march for our lives.

Far-away victims of exile wait,
undone Libyan dreams,
drought of an eastern enigma,
destroyed to feed a dream.

We have removed the mascara
of unconditional forgiveness
to face the global kill zone of this civilization's arrogance.

Help me throw rotten apples at the kepis.
Don't waste any contradictory oranges
nor sensual eggplants.
Their uniforms are deaf to the heart.

Better if we launch cashew seeds
to disactivate the intelligent weapons.
No one defends us from the promotion of agony.

Why not live to question the temptation of being happy?
We change the roses of Afghanistan
For the pistols of the contaminated water
for the excavations of evil.

Steamy, an early dew
of sensual oregano falls
over the violent memory of a military whistle
I give you a silent canteen
for the fiction of your ultimate sunrise.
There is a red stuffed animal across the innocent game
of killing us until the end
on behalf of toy lead soldiers.

We march against the idiotic dolls
They whiten the skin of black girls
they celebrate the vanishing of this fake *daycare*
where the children play strength
and think bleeding electronic imagination.

There is a cloud of inoffensive rockets
aiming towards the eyes of a lizard.
The owl no longer makes love in the half-light.

We marching against the goodness in old Santa's stomach.
An eastern kingdom annoys our memories.
Neither Melchor nor the other crowned spies
are innocent of keeping so much hope awake.
There is the line of rebellious philosophers
disarmed for not playing
the game of truth in time.
History lost to its ultimate battle.

There is an urgent operating room for the heroes
that still resist a life in disaster,
Laugh at the trivialized mythologies.

183

The orphans produced by the sweat
of two waists, silent and apathetic,
still fight over a broken arm.

The report of a still breast caresses an empty head
as a desire to sacrifice an intelligent armpit
for the recuperation of some great buttocks.
There is a disgusting baby-pacifier for the archeologists of
pleasure.
The wisdom of an 11-year-old girl instructs a satrap,
the blood of a school speaks to the world.

Hopelessness believes itself lucky to be a monolingual adventure.
The press leaves sacred cameras everywhere
to combat the boredom of this corsair day.

They carry open microphones,
toy vaginas and supportive penises,
alphabetized to measure the blood of the fallen.

We march against the complicity of this epoch
preceded by devil's advocates
and sexual predators of the state
—honored by an apocryphal gospel.

This is not the end of the world yet.
They only defend us from femicides
and the official harassment of the imperial circus.

The apprentice of the Oral Office,
instead of governing for the fellow men,
combs his hair with the blood of the fallen,
while digging the tomb of his miseries
in the courtyard of an indifferent asylum
at the collapse of the niche of progress.

There is no collusion

(A children's poem for The Cursed Clown)

There is no collusion.
It matters little if I haven't read Pushkin.
My love for the Russians
didn't include reading poems
by Vladimir Mayakovsky either;
and don't be surprised if I tell the truth
—I'm yet to try Joseph Stalin's sacred wine
but I thank God and the unparalleled
America First.

There is no collusion.
The economy is strong.
Very strong, prosperous,
I have armed the world's unconsciousness.
Now you can kill legally
—we extended legal age to 21.
Even teachers can defend their chalk
with bulletproof vests and righteous guns.
The temple of knowledge
guards the pedestal of the gods.
I'm not guilty of such sensuality.
I love the torments of this logical desert,
Immune to the truth
Without dangerous mirages.

There is no collusion.
In the technological revolution,
Gutenberg is not to blame for sabotaging
priestly luxury; his press is not to blame
for so much intimate exile.
Neither are the equity owners.

There is too much innocence
in the sacred ovens of this deficit hell.

185

There is no collusion
if we question the solid
Geometry of the invertebrate uniform
The tame Math of the twilight passion
in Wall Street's gluttonous walls.
There is still medicinal science for everyone's voracity,
but there is no collusion.

Don´t be too mad or to too complacent.
Truth can no longer be proven
by looking at sunflowers.
If we are going to denuclearize feelings
who cares about the holiness
of the Establishment?
If behind any Black Lives Matter
there is a Barack Obama.
Without imperialist ambition
there cannot be collusion.

This Argentine pope is too progressive
to save civilization from Christianity's piety.
There is no collusion in the *perhaps*
Not even in a fiery *maybe.*
We can interrogate the alphabet
of this compulsory Esperanto
without the presence of a special investigator
in the promotion of deportations
if we made over two hundred million
With the Black Panther's cinematic success.

There is no collusion on the beds prior
to toilet paper's history.
There is not enough disappointment
to fill our speech.
With sharp and absurd words
There is a sick fashion show
In the *Oral* Office.

There is no collusion in Syria or Yemen.
There is also no collusion in the destruction

of the environment
or in the Palestinian protesters;
Nor in the zodiacal demolition of my house.
It doesn't hurt me to dynamite a pine tree
to blast an empty wheelchair with a missile
To fill up my ears with concrete.

There is no collusion if we institutionalize
a notion of progress and regression.
Without contradictory limits
If poetry was always unproductive
Like the luxury of clowns;
And the past and present
don't get into fist fights
Until the unexpected orchid is born
In some corner of Charlottesville
And we don't implore that, to win the fight,
your opponent must fall three times,
Or that the dreadlocks go loose
off the cursed clown's hard head.

I have not read November's orthography,
but there cannot be any collusion
if the gate keeper of the intimate law's king
suffers from being Jewish
and doesn't want to be a Philistine.

I'm not an atheist by trade either.
There are not heartfelt condolences
in the spelling of the word collusion
and even less in the present legacy
of the Saudi association.

There is no collusion in Parkland
or in the *kamasutras* of the past.
There is no collusion in the sacred condoms
of so much terrifying communion
of the mundane crimes
that embellish TV's nutrition.

We haven't overcome the duty
of living under a decisive wealth.

There is no collusion
in unpayable debts
Nor in the homeland security's initials.
Ask yourselves once again why
we launch rotten cabbages against
the cheap crosses of humble
and servile Christ-servants
of a world infected
by predatory innocence.

There is no collusion
There is no collusion

If the grapes from the benevolent beach rot
inches away from the cheeses
of the eternal alliance for progress.

There is no collusion in the Security Council
if they privatize social security
nor if they sell my health insurance
to a defamation trade.

There is no collusion
under the journey of the last Castro
nor against those *Castra*ted
by imperial bliss.

There is no collusion.

There never was.

Christ has no time to wear new clothes.
His old whip got rotten over time.

There is no collusion
if the togas fight against the monopoly
of the disastrous and cordial fashion show.

Any Sunday accumulates insufficient faith.
We spray a funeral perfume just in case
they protest too much.
I would have loved to be an architect
—a shameless importer of gargoyles.

You have to taste the monotony
of the cultural corridors
of the beautiful oppression
of the dictatorial civilization
to ignite a new thought.

There is no collusion if we get bored
with the mirage of Roman law
or if in the judicial revolution
there is a journalistic plague
and if rhetoric takes place in the heart
of the devil's advocates.

Good old Marx ignored the make-up of the circus
The insurgency of a necessary heroism.

Unfortunately, college culture has died.
There are too many centers of perdition
that celebrate culture.
They sometimes enter a classroom
to observe the cadaver of a hecatomb
reduced to 108 useless bones.

And we still can't know if there is collusion
if the rhetoric of the right to life
won't defend the honor of a panty
that pays for a hymen's secrets
—the imperial phallus is to be protected
from any catastrophe.

The femicides of tenderness
ensure the legs of a diva.
The legal truth is sumptuous;
It begins a feminist fashion

to hide a late fetus.
There is a humanitarian placenta.
We can extend the dehumanization
of the tenderness of the Negro Leagues
of the intimacy of the smoke
for a state secret.

We have the right to a "habeas corpus."

There is no collusion.
There never was collusion.

If the diplomacy of olives disappeared
from the Hispanophile
if freedom of the Press was the benefactor
Myth of neglect.

There is no collusion during this return
to contemporary prehistory.
It would be good to free myself by consuming
the silence of so much charming
and indiscreet horizontality.

It hurts me to be isolated
from so much unfathomable degradation.
I can learn to die fast.
One must defend black beans
Even If one is to adopt the red ones later.

And then I opt to keep some
of the white ones
for an angelical orgy.

Maybe the remnants
of hopelessness
can be rescued.

190

Oh, CUNY, I cannot breathe

If they resell my neurons on consignment,
there is a payable check book to question indifference,
a virtual chalk, a desk outside the book,
and a uniformed discussion of the slave's deficit
peace observed every semester.

Since yesterday the dreamer gave way
to the creator; The teacher gave birth to suicide.
He still laughs if someone questions the silence.
True teaching was always illegal. And trivial
was tithe and the scrupulous commendation.

There's still a clever room to celebrate Monday's
bliss, Tuesday's death. There are 24 hours
of anguished Corsair joy. There is a sordid week
to applaud the one who graduated from being happy.

I cannot deny this longing for lost days
and drunken nights of corporate oppression.
This statement of uncertainty cannot breathe.

Yesterday was an inorganic Tuesday,
blatantly tacit. I can't fight the wandering
memory of this gloriously infamous day.

In the days leading up to the pedagogical theater
you can only breathe a smell of dead flowers
and another petrified feeling of poetic exhumation.

I can no longer invent the resigned beauty
of another genocide to convince the Pope
of liberal education that he can still desist from
by defending my virtual kitchen
and the immoral exile of this daily cry.

Without understanding the emptiness, I wait
a day to make up the skin on the blackboards.

The minute of silence of my death was 6 years
old, but I celebrate his forgetful bliss.
We throw the house out the window
so that the fireplace breathes the seductive
perfume of monotonous chalk.

Today the lung of the day flatters
another intelligent disease,
invents a sedentary smoke
But tastes a pedagogy of happy atrocity.

So much right to celebrate duty feeds disappointments.
You can call the pardoned on presidential day.
There is no constitution for disobedient lungs
and no fallen arms for anti-diluvial hope.

It is not yet known whether there is any ink left
to resist duty. Or if the stolen pen and romantic
white chalk advance toward another colonization
of tenderness, or if the agony of duty conspires
to impose a famine of miserable intelligence.

The walls proclaim a perverse transparency
But education fails to moralize the migratory
apathy of zombies that jump all day.

This progress breeds distrust.
Other weeks of useless migrations return
To a slate that militates in the desert.

The blue day lacked more badges,
the night stopped breathing its gray whiteness.
There is too much chastity in this love.
The description of this ridiculousness ceased
to segregate a migratory rainbow.
I am not afraid to know if the ashes
of this educational crematorium
so luxurious and absurd, has the certainty
that this perfumed genocide is no longer anonymous.

SIGHTSEEING IN THE VALLEY OF THE FALLEN

(New York, 2019)

Translated by Erin Mangan, María Postigo, & Luke Johnson.

Sightseeing in the valley of the fallen

Everything is laughable —with the same laughter
and seriousness of any *performance;*
And we do it with pleasure although
they humiliate us with pain when they open
the doors of this lapidary paradise.

There is sweet puss in our hands
to use as challenging makeup.
It's a shame, dear reader, that you can't savor it.
It is the anonymous honey of the great judgment.

An invertebrate memory leads its march
towards Hell. My orphanhood awaits on the edge
of another food Purgatory to starve the soul.
We militate in a garbage dump tormented
by contempt. The cats export our dreams into
a box of political and apocalyptic surprises.

But a culprit was missing
—a cheap excuse for the independent press
"To save the healthiest Circus amusement."

The free dog of the first world is too loyal
to be able to understand its humiliating destiny.
I'm the one with the second silent Armageddon.
I only bark to exercise the strings of my pride
and charge cash for being my master's canine clown of love.

Most of the day I thrive on two crutches
Or drag a walker or a wheelchair.

The others crawl to rip off footsteps
from the world. I amuse the babysitter
with my colossal jumps
and my incomprehensible obedience offends the proud.

195

I am the laughter therapy of the infidels.
I buried my identity in a poem.
They stole my contest of pleasure.
The jury that discarded my calligraphy
died before they gave me the verdict.

I bet my nightmare in the sanctuaries
of unfulfilled duty. I ignore myself if
they banish me from this residence in the shade.
The ramparts of insulting judgment try to stop
my steps, but don't imprison me enough.
They are too old to contain the imagination
of this endless pain without avenged cameras.
From kissing them so much, they already inhabit our hearts.
You are the one from the third world, my son.
You, laughing at your own misery,
end up celebrating them like the bleak triumph
of the endless folklore of the era.

You are good at losing elections or at getting
condemned to death and to silence.
You praise your suicide with fervor,
Taking care of a bank that undercapitalizes
your reasons; Or do you keep assaulting yourself
to devour the goods of your demoralization?

You're another Góngora on a *motoconcho*

I thought you were a drunk Góngora
willing to challenge your laughter,
savor your tears and celebrate not
having killed your doubles on time.
Or the Siamese guy who create your nights
of calculated pleasure
and without judging the failure to arrive
in time to the destination
of those guilty of existence or of walking
through the city with practical sense

You know no more delight than kneeling
in the face of political rot. They took away
the impossible questions, the harlot words,
the bliss devoured by the laughter of this voluntary manslaughter.

You love the honor and dignity of being
the number-one slave. Hidden among the resigned,
you get lost among the masses
that feed the most immune Caesars.
He who, one day, gave up on saving himself
from the apathy of sweetness.
It doesn't matter if they call you
Mumias or Mandela. You once were perhaps
a shadow of Angela Davis or a child raped
by a disavowed tourist in the middle of the night.

No one knew if your sexual preference
made sense or if sexual ambiguity made
you a victim
—or a hero floating in the embarrassment
of another medieval moral crisis.

You should speak all the languages of pain
but don't dare to decode that of unclean crying.
You know the language of smoke,
and that of the zodiacal sign of silence.

197

Sometimes you play mute or a dogmatic parrot
and drown a parrot within you.
A useless bloodhound in the mood for dawn
being the sausage of grateful beggars.
A sultan, awake all night by the spit
of some god without feminine memory.

They come more fallen by dragging
the semantics of the verb fall.
Add themselves to a monotone syntax.
One feels like expelling the textbook
on feeling like inaugurating a treacherous morphology.
Avoid its intimate reading.
The fallen do not read from the field of inertia.

I kindly ask for another insurmountable agony.
A noble human waste, a proud obstinacy.
The offensive wisdom of the fallen weighs
down the guilt of the last spoiled satrap.
Take it away from other's dreams again.
Experience the tormenting luxury
            of devouring your roots.

Accuse yourself of celebrating your banishment
with a national beer in your hand.
An otherness without a term or a doubt.

And say it so that your remains can hear it:
I'm the starchy man, the tourist mouse
in the pockets. Sigh for your digital absence.

You were an autumn without a bed book.
The library accepts only consecrated souls.

Champions of a seductive dumbing-down.
The dead applaud your last fall.

You go out into the distribution of your organs,

inaugurating a civilized lust to respond to the power of lies.
Vomit again. Here is an unarmed bust at your service.

They stole the uniform from the statue
of your tears and melted its mandatory
weapon to amuse a dictator.

There is a silent mass of those fallen off motorcycles,
fallen who run showing off their muscles,
fallen who smoke the pipe
of a war that was never holy,
a move without wage or menstrual progress.

All of us who are fallen are prisoners
of this sacred mess. We squander rancor,
squander hatred, and there is no trophy
to taste the ultimate taste of hopelessness.
You were vanquished by promises.

The pharmacies were there
ready to shoot at the masses.

The hospital welcomed you and made love to you.
It let you go in without a shirt and you
left as the great tourist sick of his liberating theories.
You were the homeless clown or the hungry doll.
You no longer found a credible mask in the middle of the dark.

Identify your fingerprints.
Record them on empty headstones
and the decorative cemeteries of the alternative future.
They are useful only to love or hide the illusion
of your own cowardice in an impotent poem.

Swear you will tell the truth about your failed triumphs.
You painted your body to unknow yourself.
No one knows you've undressed yourself of your ambitions.
You sell your organs in life.
You bury yourself alive to save the lie of this civilization.

You got lost among the ghosts
that pay to see you progress.

Smell your own stench,
photograph your faithful paradise
on the unheard sidewalk.
No one accuses you of dying bravely.
They only blame you for missing
the train of an impossible dream
or the shopping cart of progress.

A hypocritical religion wants
to take away your unanimous desire
to disappear under a tactile bomb,
so notorious, you can see it in complete disrespect.
You sleep on the edge of the bliss of a leak.

You find no other cavern besides
your own repentance.
Nothing takes away your gloomy
glow of being nobody.

Let us celebrate together the failure
of irrationality. Exercise your right
to die from the same failed act of living.
Explode once and for all after every
mistake you make toward the end
of a surprising statement of failure.
Celebrate it with fervor.

Scream. Drag your 'identity' misery.
Greet the statue of a waste,
the mist of the gods who ruined you.
Blackmail your betrayal.
You come out of the coffin to perfume the logs.
Just for the futility of a garden
of bones devoid of saltpeter.

You celebrate your trip without
any suicidal remorse.

Absurdity frees you from being healthy.
Not even Guayasamín is needed
to explain the aesthetics of your skeleton.

You get robbed while you die.
They sell you after being buried
—with premeditation and eagerness.
Your coffin is already in public auction.

You are the first to buy
your nose and kiss your mouth.

The usurers of melancholy
don't let you love yourself.
You have an island buried
in your heart and nobody cares.
Annual waves blur tenderness.
The shipwrecks return to celebrate
the sinking of dreams.
You ceased to exist because
you refused three times
but numerology won't stop
helping your duties.
You are your own Jude.
The Messiah gives no signs of recovery.
No matter who's ahead of you in this race.
You're in a car celebrated by a paper country.

It doesn't matter if you're a Raúl Mondesí.
The metaphor of an endless tale.
He did not learn his baseball in
an Agronomy school or read Marx
in an unknown city.
You came to the precariousness of the poem.

Bronx walkers don't let you sleep.
The fallen do rise
—and fall into more internal wars.

Your bedroom is as large as the world.
Candidates flee to avoid frustrating
a new political challenge.

To give it all back, including the pen,
the airfare, the accordion by mouth,
in exchange for Christ the King's paradise.
You voted for yourself and they let you rot
in a totally useless park.

The doves played the fool when
they stepped on the shoulders of an admiral.
You died before graduating in the adverbs of hatred.
You fought over being yourself, a certain death,
an unrenounceable public perversion.

Two sins condemn you.
You yourself do not know
why you refused to be black
and to think of another rainbow.
You don't know why independence
disgusts you. You couldn't pass the lie detector.
You didn't want to fill
your armpits with a superb book.

Losing yourself was the great heroism
of an absurd duty. Give up that lying skin.
Break the clocks. You speak the language of fear.
You jump out of any caravan
and don't fit in the tents of the era.

You are the grammar monkey
of an abandoned circus in the middle
of the desert. A defector signed by the
gods who infect the desire to be healthy
                              and smell good.

You like to bite rotten apples
Like the ears of a deaf pirate.
And also live in the religion of anonymity.

202

Exist to desist,
full wisdom of an ambulatory retreat.
Be the zero of a wrong
addition you never questioned.

You invite yourself to lose
so as not to disappoint contempt.
You didn't know all the chains
but were never free to give up
playing Russian roulette.
You don't need cardboard houses
like the two-legged ones of the first world.
This harakiri suits you even
if it doesn't convince you.
There are no vaccines
or three meals of humiliation.
Sometimes they make you a junkie of fear,
Just another snitch of your caresses,
a four-legged mole in the agencies of insecurity
serving the return to another exhaust valve.
Your poor education is higher than mine.
They call me fucking dog and throw
stones at me and hide with the Bank's watchmen.

The cat is another thing
if you don't read in verse anymore.
Prose is the honey of the hungry.

The cat betrays its worldly origin
to further prolong its inner misery.
It's the terror of the daycare.
The perpetual therapy of an abyss
—it matters only as a pictorial work of a memory.

They paint it to receive poets and sell postcards.
It agonizes in the windows like an owl
committed to the stars,
as a refugee from a life too civilized
to be once again the hunter of its own death.
The dog is an instrument of perdition

—of the big consumer society.

The two accomplices are the therapy
of those who only love themselves.

The dog always brings the bone
to the master and even sleeps in
his bed for three meals a day
and a suspicious vaccine.
It won't stop giving birth
so the master can sell its children
to buy a pipe (that will never be the pipe of peace)
and to lose the couple in the park.
It is the police who denounce
the trafficker with his vanity.

Better leave in a hurry
to avoid the false tenderness
of the other fallen.

They block the way of those
with clean nails. They fill Paradise
with unprecedented venereal diseases.
Happy to distance themselves
from their latest masks.
They offend the remnants
of clumsy imagination
that still survive as we escape
the emphasis of that sordid frustration.

The dehumanized culture
marches backwards to its darkness.

The house of knowledge closes
its eyelids referring to the research
centers of its destiny.

No rebellion justifies the landscape
Of their last illness.
They are the sacred wastes of history.

The horse is a simile of the cruelest questions.
Wrecked cars make fun of them.
Modernity freed the horse, but its remains
rest in any city alley to feed flies, rats, birds
of prey that pass by in their luxury carts
to legislate on the fate of the next tree.

They go on to manage despair
with pride, sometimes with a breed dog,
or a beautiful cat that gives therapy
to those whose profession is to analyze.

Your case is different.
I invoke their benign betrayal.

It is written by other beggars
of the agony of the subway.

I returned to my semester alphabet

To the algebra of a beautiful despair,
a cursed hotel that never stops
for imaginary doctors to certify
the final deaths, the suicidal contempt
of the mourners of the distribution
of wealth. You must cry for the beneficiaries
of the growing Economy. The call only drags ties.
A tour of the cavern promotes their counter dance.
The absence of modesty remains
their most notorious prominence.

Resentment is the *daycare* of bliss.
They no longer have to report
the final Income tax.
They hate disempowered public
Accountants And are disgusted
by the lawyers who fight for the final play.
They only important role
is in the uprooting of loneliness.
They were the excuse of the bourgeois
Evolution and now the fascist revolution,
the linear freedom of the bloody doubts
and the failure of the last heartbeats
of the failed states of the soul.
They were the most lucid honey
of the spiritual crusades of hate.
The Gaza strip of a pointless comedy.

They drag a harmless dirt and are not
worthy of trust—not even from flies.

The birds flee from a kindness
disapproved by squirrels.
Towards this anonymous mass
sometimes an artist flees tired of
painting the void or a poet succumbs
with his dead metaphors toward another invisibility.

A neutrality, legalized by the atmosphere,
imprisons them until they deny
their content from breathing well.

We have been condemned to flee from mirrors.
We are a vanity whose involuntary mission
is to undo the final remnants of identity in a putrid system.
Through them our inner vanity is discovered.
We are the face that denies us.
We form some kind of seers addicted
to capsizing in the rebellion of blindness.
We have the courage to undermine desolation.
We know how to dwell on the surface
of a beautiful landfill. Or sleep peacefully
under the luxury of a rusty needle.

The rats take care of the disposable
daycare of their retirement crisis.
They no longer believe in prayers
or speeches of the end of the world.
Misery is their final fleeting freedom.
May the heirs of your forgotten
languages drink to your name.
Contempt writes its memories
Despite the hypocrisy of those guilty
of creating economy food places.
They carry the law of the simulation of fake backpacks.
They do not prevent the discovery
of the haphazard game of a millennial spoil.

They represent the antipode
of the useless slogans of those
who only stand to disguise their horizontality.
They claim to be the true tourists
of the Valley of the Fallen. They cry upside down.
Die under a struggle of opposites,
protected by the whims of power.
Your bankruptcy is the Central
Bank's unlimited return victory.

A non-profit organization
is the embassy that certifies
its expulsion into disorder.

They paint a floating lie on the surface of pain.
They live on a murky sidewalk,
privatized by a public tumor.
Addicted to seeing them disappear
below the rain, they hide at the gates
of a mundane cathedral where
the priests flee toward art and count
the bank deposit of corporate cigar
butts at the end of the day.

They taste the economic growth of destitution
as the sacred diet of the Justice Show.

If the cold condemns us to sleep
under the bliss of an emergency room,
we give enticing cries to question
the insecurity of the oppressors.

SHE IS NOT MY TYPE

(New York, 2019)

Translated by Brienna Fleming.

Predatory dictatorships

Latin-American dictatorships
Were predatory, vertical,
circular and horizontal machines.
Today we all look like Trujillo.
The laboratory is no longer
that of the children of Brazil.
Our gestures were globalized by Facebook.
Someone says it was a necessary cloning.
The sensual rumor speaks
of an extraordinary imagination.

The law of organic exchange
is a secret without fees.
The slogan was: any vagina is mine,
like the earth and the destiny of men.
Sexual preference was part of fascism.

There is a linear sex alphabet.
A reading without recurring intertexts
excludes other sexualities.
Then a joyous trigger arises.
Even the use of a hand is an official matter.
A basic math without decorum.
And a hypothetical geometry.

The position of the period does not matter.
Zeros can be to the left or to the right
of the center of misery.
The ethics of exchange is indifferent.
The day is uniformed even
when dressed in civilian clothes.

For a C, I give you my right breast
and even a visa in the Bronx,
if you go down from the navel.
For a B, I give you the left one, but be careful,
It may be linked to a right-wing Marxism

or to a fascism subjected to the other.
If I am very old with no hope of a slow death,
I will move you in with me for a kiss
and let you drain me off my savings
even in the Woodland Cemetery.

If there are still promises on layaway,
I can give you a scholarship in
an erotic kitchen or a graduate degree
if you're a pro with hot combs.
If you are black, I offer you the trunk of doubts
and the most recent fear of El Big Papi.
Baseball sovereignty is expensive.

If you are aware of your body,
I take care of the needs of your belly's profession.
The kingdom hall is yours even if you are a heretic.
The dictatorial harem may be the hope
of an unprecedented slave pride.
We are not so Muslim, Buddhist or so Jewish.
Our Christianity only admits
mandatory political crusades.
Although we have changed our motherland,
no one talks about the predators of agony.

The dead always give away their ashes
even if there is an unfaithful alphabet.
Generalissimo Rafael Leónidas Trujillo Molina,
godfather of the nation, took out the Mirabal sisters.

He had his country homes
and his well-paid women-mongers.
The public treasury had a sexual destiny outside the budget.
The streets were the familiar desert of a horizontal debate.

Fragmentary necrophilia

Sometimes we make love with a thigh.
We carry it around and shave it with honey,
we talk about the indifference of the pious ass,
and about the fear of the return of our baby teeth,
and we add the pedophilia of silly toy dolls
to the disappearance of community life.
Sometimes there is an eye that looks
at us to confirm our death.
When that happens, a woman turns
on the television while other dead
act their roles to make us believe
that the seventh art has achieved its ultimate goal:
annihilate the ashes from the slave's mask.

She is not my type

You said she's not your type.
This is not a negative concert
on the typology of oppression.
She has not said I am the chosen one
I am not the fast food of her kind.
Her subject can't be me.
She is not a possessive ruin
not even a tragic heroism
to amuse the lust for sin.
I am not the chosen torment.
I have not decided to dispossess myself.
I don't belong to myself as a shadow
Or worldly gift of a delirium.
I am not another whim of desire.
She is not the addiction of my chimeras.
I am not the tainted sovereignty.
You must confirm it: *I am not her type.*
Here the despicable one is me
I only represent a temporary failure.

Don't blame her for floating
on nothing. I am a premeditated fiasco.
I am satisfied with this urgent delirium.
I myself have become unhinged.
No one has condemned me to being a village.
She doesn't get along with my lineage.
Nor does she take refuge in my contempt.
My contempt undresses her as an object
of a funny and vile play.
Here the object to despise is me.

She is not open to becoming
the object of my selfishness.

I do not belong to her destiny.
She doesn't understand my reasons either.
I have not chosen you as the trauma

214

of my most solemn hypocrisy.
You have not chosen me foolishly.
You are not the comedy of this laughter.
 Why do you judge me? she wonders
The pain of my absence no longer thinks.

This story devours itself.

In a judgment that does not involve me
my words do not deserve to name you.

I am not your negro

A tribute to James Baldwin

Postmodernity came, settled, rooted in the privacy of the black kingdom of the Bronx, the place where a white driver beautifully insulted me. He shouted an irrefutable *Maldito Negro* at me with the sad intention of attacking the one who still obeys the 25 miles-per-hour speed limit, imposed in the imaginary paradise of 2019's slowness. On Webster Avenue I not only knew that I was a forgetful Black man, without ceasing to be amazed at that divine poetic regeneration. If someone happens to seduce me by saying: *You are my negro*, I think about it seriously and, if it is during an innocent sexual act, I do not feel nostalgic for *brown* nor am I invaded with the fear of being white. Sexuality and love discovered the real identity of exile but we don't pay any attention to either. We are metaphysical black people. Today's sexual predators would never attack their victims with the world's deadliest weapon: *This land is not yours, Black*. Although I feel like telling you: *I am not your negro*. True beauty only dies in the courts of horizontality. If you spread your legs in time, voluntary genocide aims for a pyrrhic victory. Not even you can defend yourself from the wish of dying with your boots on.

I unfold myself

I unfold myself to make
the most interesting theater of absence possible.
I can be the unbearable *incredible* man,
a reportable sketch
or I act like one of the many inverted
vaginas out of the monologue, any Messaline,
one of the victims of the rolling theater of power
or one of the infinite ambiguities devoid of a face.
No woman accuses me of sexual harassment.
I suffer from withdrawal.
My Alzheimer's is not totally presidential.
I have not had my first circumcision.
I am not the president of any non-profit
without unspeakable profit motives.
I have no shares in the stock market
of any incurable lender.
There are not enough hitmen
Willing to pay for my silence.
I am not (and I have no reason to)
wearing their mask and go back
to being the great comedian of decorum.
I cannot embarrass Black people
nor make white people laugh
with my creative genius harassment-proof.
I'd have six lives left if I was possessed
by a mythological cat.
The West is full of Egyptian cats
and pyramids that have not been examined
by the customs officers of Purgatory.

No drone watches over this cynical hacking.
Islamic bullying is not like Christian one.
The woman is secretly crucified
but since there is complicity,
there are enough tears for the day of sacrifice.
Public lashing represents caresses of a greater degradation.

217

Stonings have not been totally banned.
Nor have machetes or bats.
Gym religion fuels that force.
There are fundamentalist kidnappings.
Missing kisses. Sensual tortures.
The flagellation of the hymen
is a necessary myth—A cult
of the macho liberated
by the consecration to freedom.
The gods feed on the blood of girls.
They buy and sell them on a whim.
I am so lucky.
No woman has written a book
to denounce my spectacular deceptions,
especially when I play the sheep man.
My hand dies on an indifferent
Knee and revives on any grave.
I can love myself without anyone knowing.
I summon the woman who inhabits me
and the man who flees from me at night,
the one who can't stand my absolute nakedness.
No woman has lied to save me
from many decades of hypocrisy.
Jean Carroll hasn't accused me yet.
Revenge is still fictional.
The illiterate save the cannibals of spirit.
Their interviews continue to ignore the Bronx.
This is the black kingdom of all questions.
Here women carry a home on their shoulders
that suffers from the termite of paradise.
There is no transsexual who accuses me
of writing a bisexual poem.
I do not accuse myself of being
a failed state of phallic culture.
I believe myself to be the silver
masked man even if the bullets are dummies.
And no Indian accompanies me.
The Lone Ranger questions
the legitimacy of the Black.

I'd like to trade my pistol for a toy one.
I am a dangerous pacifist.
My thoughts are warmed
by the ankles of any spurned Cinderella,
I donate the chains and applaud the tattoo
of any invertebrate misfortune.
I fly towards the Ursa Major
if the neck hides some lapidary gold.
I suffer from other presidential
Metamorphoses or of a body
that dies in the wrong place.
I have big and wise hands,
 the waist does not count even if it is wide.
I have firm the waist of the orgy.
It chilled the murderer's chest.
If he dies, I pay his past due bills.
My knees hurt from so much
fishing in a raging river.
I released Mike Tyson
from the electric chair.
His fists had no identity consciousness.
I saved him from an innocent biography.

He was not totally Black.

I wasn't totally mulatto either
to believe myself the target
of a sweet oppression.

The police complaint has not yet arrived.
The courts are dying to question me.
They have not examined the hard evidence
of so much frustration.
The television is empty of me.
The radio does not criticize my silences.
The great judge of the president,
He beat an innocent woman.
They only accuse the clown of hiding
that I am not a judge
accused of sexual harassment.

Political parties will be
centers of sexual harassment
where the withdrawal of a judge
nor the referendum of a glance
is not discussed.
It's that being a woman
is still a matter of a burning chapel
or should we wait for 50 to come,
or 60 to face crime of a handshake,
an unexpected caress below the navel.
No one accuses me of postponing an orgasm
to read an innocent poem of their doubts.
I'm not Lorena Bobbit to be a waste
of deficit television
or a phallic triumph of a Show Man
of the laughter lottery;
I'm not the heroine of the military penis
 with the right to reply either.

They touched me in a border daycare,
the concentration camp was not
between the glutes of a slogan
without inevitable desires.

I swear in front of the supreme
Court of theoretical injustice.
I was not a lover of Bill Clinton.
I'm not even Paula Jones's cousin.
In 2016, I couldn't vote for the first lady.
Monica Lewinsky should be compensated for life.
Horizontality was prohibited in the White House.
I was there for academic reasons.
I didn't know that he was president either
of a Federation of defenseless beings;
I was not a lover of Michael Dukakis
let alone Richard Nixon.

I didn't know that he was absent
from the electoral slaughterhouse.

I am a pedophile priest for the love of God.

By his mercy I came to Poland
to die without being absolved
for the innocence of my victims.
The postmodern inquisition
tells the fear to the court.
There are no hitmen in the Holy See
nor in the cages of border children.

Many will never see their parents again.

Necrophilia of flesh and copper

She returns to lost paradise from a quick meal and a community garden, full of white butterflies. The saint awaits her from his metallic life, standing, firm, on the same pedestal in the Amsterdam garden, looking down on intruders. As her lover escorted her through the grove, haunted by a suspicion, she ran after the wisdom of a beggar. She kissed his rags. She left her lover behind. Nobody was interested in the mystery of the death certificate of the saint. Her state of health was optimal. It was a tribute to the libertarian and apocalyptic life of a redemptive hedonism. He surrounded the garden of the cathedral of mortgaged art. He questioned it with all his senses. He reviewed the story of the demon with a severed head inside the dry fountain and kissed the feet of a Christ the Redeemer distracted by the absence of his first crucifixion. Faced with the inability of the Son of God to resurrect in front of her beauty, she hurriedly fled to the garden of a daycare. There was the saint waiting for her with open arms and the graceful coin from his bare chest in the open air. Her blue trousers, torn from the knees, painted a desirable woman's spoil and the magnanimous, accustomed to sacrifice, allowed himself to be seduced by her sovereign hands and by the promptness with which she decided to explore the sensual copper of his hot skin. When the statue of that apocryphal Christianity tried to escape to the world of the living, the passion of the copper stopped it with the burning little bird seducing her hands. She tried to pray, but he wouldn't let her. His lips took over the helpless flapping, preventing the bird from his last flight.

TROPICAL BARILOCHE

(New York, 2019)

Translated by Lexi Fox.

Bariloche

Open yourself again.
Let the world fit in your mouth.
Make so much peace hurt.
Close our eyelids.
Let yourself die from the heat.
Do not return from that absent bliss.
Savor the migratory
whims of this senseless stay.
There are salted
Metaphors still undeciphered.
Go fasting to compose
this hymn without a homeland.
Raise this useless flag.
Make Bariloche tropical again.
Now a palm tree grows
under the Caribbean winds.

The fire of a match

I look you over before we make love.
My sensory neurons activate.
I discover another theory of desire.
You are the fixed point of a black mole.
A useless piece of knowledge triumphs.
He was supposed to sing to you
with a bibliography
to devour his derivatives.
So we bet on six
with another stable head
and I was falling in a delicious abyss.
I do not understand myself as a duty.
The ethics of desire are a misfortune
of irreproachable surprises.
I will continue looking you over
to imagine you. I want you
to live a phallic crisis.
Sing to me in your tongue.
Do it with your hands. Scare me.
Seduce me with your emotions.
Transgress forms, uninhabit gender!
Let´s not accommodate ourselves
to the history of the sexuality of oppression.
I cannot touch myself in the temple
of fatuous knowledge.
The taunt of a gargoyle is missing.
To recuperate lucidity
there are sensual Pharisees.

I will accompany you
even if you do not know it.
I leave you so that you love yourself.
Discover other moans.
Open yourself to other ways
We are entering another world.
Inhabit me, please.
Do not let me think. Take it carelessly.

226

Do not question anything.
It is your destiny. Face it.
Let me see your soul
taking the flight of the owl;
Smell me again.
I must obey the gods of instinct.
I will not come out from the deep.
Love yourself while I descend.
Take off your wings proudly.
Imagine it. I will be there.
Surrender yourself.
Later tell the story
of this genocide
For me to love myself too
on the fire of a match.
When I escape from here,
tell him everything is his.
Chain yourself to his desire.
I will do it with the writer of this story.
Hold both of your hands.
He sings his tremor
as you contemplate.

Enjoy your knees for him.
He will look you over
another time to write you again.

We are in line

We are in line,
but the rails betray us.
Write: 'I'm waiting for you'
at another station
while the train occupies
the center of desire.
Love waits far on the edge
of my heart. I hear other rails.
And I feel the edge
of their sharp machetes.
They unleash sparks.
They seduce the wait.
I wait for you.
A soft rumor arrives
—of other rails
fueled by desire.
I continue here and there
questioning writing,
kissing your memory,
feeling the commotion
of this morning when
other doors open
but no other alphabet comes
or you stand among ghosts
that play at sending
the last message
of this journey of goodbyes.

This island is not for sale

We speak another language.
I speak an inorganic one.
The sanguine alphabet
shelters a garden of vowels
where a finger groans;
The skin hurts
—where the wet consonants sleep.
To my right sits the elbow
of invertebrate love.
The afternoon of the muted train
transports our bones toward
another lucid caress.
The belly comes then
over the eyes of a thigh.
I meditate on the virtue
of a sweet secretion.
It hurts to do it outside.
Other moons see us.
Snow falls on the top
of a wrong breast.
I light a cigarette;
The airy smoke savors
the speech of the armpit
The milk that we drink
Is so warm and black
And the dreams swim;
other moans float;
yesterday screams against today,
demands the bewilderment of other limbs.

I let myself be kissed on the fate
of an intelligent hymen.
Your arms save a fear
from indifferent grievances.
There are children that cry
and the wind brings grapes without promises.

Open, hang on, move the craving
towards unscrupulous greed,
savor this strange alphabet,
decolonize the goodbye,
let yourself be seduced by the hieroglyphics
of the painted bodies
dissolved in sweat
of a terror without reservations,
enter the land of doubt;
they are good to think of your body.
There is a horizon where semen
tastes like a woman,
and candles to see your sandals
and mosquitos to remember
the sweet monopoly
of your knees
while I wait for you
below the island that's not for sale.

You will write on my body

We still can save the skin
from its delicious boredom.
Let's follow the fallen without the cross
to study the geography of a secret
hidden in the confines of an elbow.
We will write a sacred poem
about the hypocrisy of the scream.
I will escape again
from these questioning rails.
We will sing the poem
of a nomadic peace.
On your forehead we will write
a raging discourse about the loneliness
of this unsustainable orgasm.
We will suffer from other whims
We will put the chalk aside
to be able to dislodge the thoughts
of useless colonizations;
And I will be obedient again.
We will make a polyglot love
on the monolingual memory
of another worldly skin,
darker and shinier.
If the assassins persecute us,
my head still remembers
your perfumed hair.
And the rain of a memory.
Any end will be useless
to nourish your infinite skin.
Recite an organic poem
where only the teeth read.

A deaf language will cry.

There is an intelligent daycare
under the tree of your legs.
We discover other seeds

There is a graceful language.
If the index lasts, you will notice
the seduction of the rainbow.
We will inhabit the last silhouette
of an improvised desire.
Other bodies are already returning.
Tired of knowing themselves,
they jump over agonizing islands.
The ancient entrails
of this dawn without you are afloat.

POETIC QUARANTINE

SOME POEMS OF 2020

(New York, 2020)

Translated by Lexi Fox.

Viral nightmare

Another Cinderella sees her last epitaph.
She trembles when she sees the windows.
In the morning she leaves her room to laugh,
jumps over a pile of dirty laundry,
goes down a hallway illuminated
by candles without Saints.
On her way to the refrigerator
Of condensed milk.
There are remains of a house in disarray.
She walks about it alone
—her cat is not around anymore.
She looks at the cold radiator aglow.
Later she returns to the room of plastic covers.
She turns off the lights to strike a match.
I hear her talk to the island map.
The inside island does
not respond to her questions.
She does not call the receiver of dead dreams.
She calls the sick one—of the March star.
She comes back out
and then tours the daycare.
She cleans the wheels of the buses.
There are no workers singing in Spanish.
She goes over the waiting room alphabet,
counts to ten around the crib
and decides to bathe the white dolls.
Spiderman coughs sitting on his throne.
She is not scared if he spits on Superman.
From the pedestal of a deceased the cat jumps.
Up above, Donald Duck's entire family.
There is a virus knocking on the door
of Walt Disney's innocent business.

He puts the mask on his photo.
The runaway children of the exile
of cradles without pacifiers cry.
The border gate hammock is activated.

She spins a pink rag doll all day long.
A baby coughs loudly.
The car of the future is empty.
A brown bear agrees to put on a mask
that belongs to a love-sick person.
Outside cries a pine the song
of the birds of an incestuous spring.
The ambulances pass without stopping.
A skateboard waits in front of a silent door.
We can hear an insistent bell ring.
They released the letters of the month
over the garden of the abandoned car.
Fumigators bombard the air,
officials of a false rainbow,
but she never gets out of the fire.

Grandfather

If the virus continues its slaughter in abundance,
feeding on whatever caress, when the glassy saliva
falls on the skin of silence,
like a drop of microscopic diamond,
it is not important if it arrives through a prodigal child
or a member from the pleasure
of some deserter's genealogy.

Now it turns out the foundations of origin are in danger.
Who will discover warm water?
Who will take me to virtual school?
Who will say tenderly:

'Hello, grandpa,
Can you take me to the park of imagination once again?
Who will tell us how the world was before this last pandemic?'

Social distance

Your body and mine
were separated by the sensual
nanotechnology of financial terror
and the predators' lack of modesty.

The silent statue of liberty
and the wall of all melancholies
were separated by the hard exile
of a virulent patriotism.

For the human condition of torment
it is good to hurry the little death
with your capricious hands
to save the famine of desire.

An ambiguous hiatus burns
asking for your thirsty mouth,
creating a mysterious sweetness in the waist.

Your gentle eyes were joined
by a starry virus—seducer of a vengeful silence.

To your shoulderless blouse,
the saliva of a funeral virus
and the judicious innocence of the navel.

To the historic sickle and hammer
of indifference, a laughing key
of remote shamelessness.

To your deaf pants
the blindness of my fingers
and the permanent revolution
of my hungry pockets.

Breaking News!
The frozen rain of goodbyes arrived

238

and the horizontal poem
of a happiness devoid of chimeras got cold.

The virus of your tired eyelids
was defeated by an innocent tear.

The tinder pine spared us
from the springtime surprise
and the song of the crows was a dark fate.

The rumor of fear caresses the smoky wind
and a street -empty of us-closes all the catwalks.

Neither the asphalt (accomplice of a break),
an unscrupulous grave,
nor the resistance of laurels
can possibly imagine this victory.

To the fiery dead of thought,
other magical flowers greet the madness of absence.

The courtyard of the underhanded future
has days left militarized
by the protagonists of this pious quarantine.

To the traitorous anguish, the love of this curfew;
and the ridiculousness of horror leaves us without attributes.

To the restless haze of grief there are the closed doors
of a heart desperate to stop being linear.

And then so many questions
outside the blackboard: No one offers a response.

Innocent game

When we really relax
and you don't laugh at the lack of promises
of this last-minute lapidary poem,
the virus of 2020 flees from beauty.
It can't stand that you've been to the notary
or that you sleep in ignorance of the certainty
of the six-feet of distance rule.
I suggest that, to attack him with beauty,
we dress like the minstrel of the hospitable crown.
Like those who don't know where their mother
has died or where the cat of the residual therapies awaits.
Do not be confused by the fear of this condemnation,
tide of anxiety. Call someone to decipher the wish.
Paint the fear of a state psychopath.
Throw baseballs at the unspoken face.
Erase that aggressive laughter with
a pitch that hits on the origin of it.
Put the tail on the monster with
your eyes closed or make a spectacular goal.
Now that the stadiums suffer from cancer,
the metamorphosis of a toy hospital.
Visit death with a red flower.
Write a poem for the inmates of this speculative quarantine,
Made up to undo the identity of this blissful global decay.
Don't celebrate having lived through this phallic era.

Do not let them ruin your party.

You are no longer a minor.
Let us make up a silly joke.
The spectacular story of a healthy
Eden that may save us from psychological oppression.
A ridiculous formula made Toilet-paper shortage
Fashionable and the hope of a closed street.
Name me the heir of your most
intimate assets in exchange for reading
this poem in a nap of this wrongful quarantine,

And, since tenderness is a ridiculous look,
help me finish this vital rescue.

We can run around a cardinal point
a house empty of irrational hugs
a Ridiculous and beautiful boredom
without ping-pong to feed childhood.
Kiss the clouds. Pose decontaminating
The route of birds of prey.

If you die before some
confusing cough of a disposable lung,
remember this desert.
I wrote it for you and for all
the anonymous distrustful pronouns.
They have not been sentenced
by sadness to tour the laughter-house.
The demolition fair of progression is missing.
Hurry up. There is no time to lose.
Throw any "dead cow"
at the super clown of dissolute wealth.
We still have options to play target shooting,
sometimes injustice works or we hand
you a weapon jealous of the future:
Russian roulette of a bohemian afternoon.

The laughter of the children arrives at school
of the crashed virus inside your own "home".

The crime lab militates in its own room.
They helped me regain my sanity from this virulent daycare.

Your name is Jonathan

Wake up, son. Don't let them put you back to sleep. Recover the lucidity of will. Don't accept the apocalyptic conjugation of falling asleep's past tense. Free science does not conform to the ideologic rules of dreaming. That of the mercenaries pretends to be ambivalent. The extermination lapidaries don't stay at home. Your roots don't stay in the laboratory of pain. Your will questions the organic dream. Do not worry about the awakening of hopelessness. You are too rational to have your willingness travel to the birth of life suppressed. It is not your fault. Days and nights of love pass, but you do not wake up in time with your sacred mask. You cannot take a selfie to know how you sleep, and I, to think about the deserters of the mystery. You can't help but be the pet of a dubious return. It is not a tacit death sentence. There is no free electric chair or comfortable bed to voluntarily put you to sleep. Still you have the early reprieve of an experimental dream. The sadness of late childhood follows you. You are no longer the income taxpayer of Mount Hope or the son of the Landlord's house. Your mother gave up the twilight's exile to protect the dawn. Your body never knew about miraculous pandemics or merciful quarantines. You didn't get the chance to enjoy quarantine as afternoon therapy on Grand Concourse. You don't even remember childhood monolingualism, when you were forced to speak 'English without barriers.' There was a time when playing with your food was not a dangerous exorcism. Any famine in diapers could be utopian. There was another time in which the past tense of 'there is or there was' was nonsense. You didn't know how to speak the Portuguese of love for Ignacio Lula da Silva.

Now you can translate the hope of Fernando Pessoa directly into English, without Google or needing to go on a 15-day Safari without knowing whether you had a wife or parents... or a brother when they turned you into a masterpiece of a horizontal laboratory. You were a simple experiment on the right to life, tormented by the repetitions perhaps of the *Children Hospital*. Now you can truly live, as the final hypothesis of the condemned to be free from an uncertain destiny. You have only two alternatives: Do you send the virus to surrender its memory to Fort Apache in the Bronx or defend yourself against your own weakness? You couldn't sustain the statistics of the African-American groups that were never black. However, they can tolerate being natives of the shadows, if there is an exodus from Evo's Bolivia or from colonial otherness in America. Fortunately, you have already recovered the identity of the prehistoric man. You already know where you come from and suspect who you were from the sequence of the last 30 days. Your name is Jonathan. Remember?

Metamorphosis of agony

Perhaps nothing is the same. I am not the teacher, the dad, the driver of an ambulance. I am not the landlord nor the supervisor of misery. Neither am I an adjunct from 1986. I became a residual company. In a network of spells. I am no longer *the homeless*. I am the freed man who drags the old chains into the sea. I am other people. The consciousness of a suicide. The dead who think they are not disposable. There is a dialectic of pain, if a ship is not a ship. Let's not trust the virtue of Churches. Some have morphed into dubious cemeteries, federal reserves, a house of heretical art, a sanctuary for suicide bombers, or liberal theaters of another era or stinking hospitals of non-transferable beauty. A jail no longer serves to despise freedom or to imprison doubts or free us from the death penalty. The prisoners must be released so that they do not die of this. Home has been turning into a prison for a long time. Other gallows germinate inside. The death penalty allowed to go out and save the moor. We died *en masse* in solitude that was consuming the remains of the home. It took a virus to believe that we are alive. The civilized man is too intelligent to give up his independence. He evolves into another prehistory. A virtual jungle that thrives on the dimensions of distance.

Pandemic sun

Now the blind can see its absence.
In vain did Mr. Sun came out again.
I wonder if this scenario is adequate
to pass a smart urine test.
No one allows dialogues
with the toilet paper from another
era of liberal lintels or sleeping on
the avenue of progress or hitting
heavy balls into the golden glove
of daddy's son. Maybe we ought
to clean the yard of lost baseballs in the last decades.
I feel that today is not a good day
to die uselessly, facing the rays of
a wasted sun, nothing is salty or creeping.
It is necessary to die under a different landscape.
There is a reason to denounce spring.
It is not worth accusing her of such
beauty worn in the disappearance of our gaze.
Maybe there is a moratorium in the operating room.
Someone gets up again and refuses to die
of their own free will. He had the courage
to refuse and then breathed again.
I hear other ambulances from the previous night.
Instead of bachatas and accordions,
fire trucks were the childhood romance
of goodbye. Other ambulances rang incessantly again,
dragging the silence of a damp morgue
in the midst of an absurd discretion;
I thought of you again. The mask fixed
on your face like the latest pandemic comedy.

BLACK POEMS

A QUEST FOR BLACKNESS

(New York, 2020)

Translated by Carley Mills.

Brave cane

I spell your first name in the sand.
It is sweet, firm and straight.
The machetes knock it down
mercilessly. I bleed for you.
You await my sweat.
There is a sensual harvest
for soundless days. Sing with me.
I wait in the museum of coffee to
decolonize my nostalgia.
Accompany me.
I wait for you in a port where
you won't be free either.
The cry of the drums scares Paradise.
Dance your pain on my skin.
Serpents greet the song of your hands.
Move your feet with the glow of your waist.
I kiss your skin to quench my thirst.
We are real black.
May the memory of others
who are not black never protect us.
You resist in a village where happiness
has no more modesty
than the extermination of the sea.
Inhabit me. You sleep on the sand
of my hands. You swim to undo
the remains of this sweet anguish.

Letter to court a fugitive king

How fortunate I am. We chilled our coffee and drank tears of love's social distance. She dreamed of that salty water of sensual sadness. We hung out without a Virgin Mary to ruin our desire to sin firmly. It is curious, King Juan Carlos flees from Spain. My fictitious memory says that he holds 500 years of mortuary citizenship. For none of his crimes will he ever be deported. His extradition would be utopian. The oligarchy pardons him. Locking him up in La Victoria for his war crimes ordered by the Catholic kings would be a mistake from Luis Abinader and Donald Trump's era. There are no insular judges for an inverted colonial court. If the distinguished king at least read a poem by Antonio Machado or brought us a black statue of Federico García Lorca, we would doubt that he is a double invertebrate nobleman. We do not know where the humble king hides his treasure. Nor where he decorates a room with the murdered stuffed animals of an innocent jungle. Read in the past tense the following present: he is so close to us, and our land is so absurd, it gives shelter to his scepter. His crown shines. He welcomes the horses of the Apocalypse from a secret soirée in Punta Cana. The vultures of the story say: Leave him alone. He returned to retrace his streets in search of his most perverse roots. They will laugh at the colonial altar of the first city of America, while you cry, while you say I love you and I say I love you or I take a selfie in the middle of squares where we have not made love, preserved apartments to greet the Catholic kings of the europhilia that return for the fingerprints of beautiful oppression. My otherness walks like a zombie, looking for the bloody corner of an *Encomendero*.

In my land there is still no pathway to interrogate the perversity of the slave business they called Encomienda, nor a meek bible to illuminate the crosses of a crusade of headless white and black militancy men, while I kiss your tears and the idolatry of Borges does not matter so much to me, nor whether or not he can be mimicked (in the words of Vargas Llosa), nor if they expelled my blackness in El Salvador in 1932 for being Afro-descendant, when, simultaneously, the white Creole dictator, Rafael Leonidas Trujillo Molina, father of the new country "discovered" by the unspeakable admiral—another defender of the agreeing white man who today helps King Juan Carlos defend the legitimate dynasty of his roots. The magnanimous man fled to the land that Columbus loved the most to humiliate it. Despite the old idyll, the ruffian king hid for a few days in the United Arab Emirates. That's what they say. He does not run away from the memory of the genocide. We have not decided to disinfect Bartolomé or Diego streets nor have we questioned the virus of 500 years of historical orgy. The ghosts of the Caravels of Terror, an empty mansion of our shadows, are still sold in the Alcazar, while I search for Marco Polo's map to disinfect it from colonial audacity or discover a mercenary Atlas. I see Américo Vespucio preparing the yellow guide to the Tordesilla treaty, measuring the limits of the Sea of Colombus followers. There are so many of them we must laugh. Let's take a break, woman, Covid 19 is not going to find out, so kiss me in front of the hotel where the last Bourbon dynasty is hidden. Kisses scare away misery and, sometimes, a decolonizing tear floods the Ozama River. In its waters float the bloody secrets of the Encomenderos and the false church of the 11th century. It was necessary to salt the fish this morning, although this king does not flee from the virus like the meditations of the king of Morocco. They say that he flees to recover his strength in the Canary Islands and not as the king of Thailand. He grows up with the virus: There are 20 concubines waiting for him to celebrate his anonymity. An island is a confessional secret that nobody cares about. There is no Advent sermon against the king of real estate nostalgia or a decree declaring Hispanophilia an incurable disease of the 21st century— as disastrous as the current Anglophilia that also helps whiten the business of childhood.

Wicked pardon

I forgive my hands
my body
my laugh
my fingers
my hair
...relics from the cemetery of consumption

I float in my infinite walking closet
I forgive this humiliating whiteness
I forgive my feet
my legs
which in times of crisis took me to play golf
(After a slaughter fest, playing golf
is a beautiful thing.)
The others did not betray my desire
to wage a trade war against my allies
to save politics from boredom
I forgive my eyes just for seeing
the beauty of evil, also my voice
my head
my brain
my ears
my nails
I danced with these organs the dance of the sword
I saved a genocide from its semantic falsehood
Yemen was a secret Armageddon
The pandemic hides its continuous fall
I am excited to kill indiscreet rivers
bless the misery of the sand
I forgive the joy on my face
I once thought I was perfect

—I love the mirrors that hide my soul

I always won the lottery of laughter.
I managed it even when I lost my humor.
It was perfect to circumvent the fiscal deficit.

252

I only loved myself.
I sang to myself as the last invertebrate
but I did not celebrate myself
like Walt Whitman did.
I despise the poetry
of his humanitarian vagrancy
the novel
the art
the music
the gypsies
the poor
I forgive the light that illuminates crying.
I, who was born under the fascism
of darkness, adore my thirst to own it all.
I forgive the common sense of my nose
I'm so despicable to flaunt this appearance
of being someone, this false sense
of being incomprehensible.
I forgive the absence of my heart.
All previous organs failed me.
I decided to exonerate them of innocence.
By the way, I hate doctors, the socialist popes,
Scientists, laboratories, sexy nurses...
I can't stand masks
—They can protect the enemy.
I do not forgive the workers
nor the southern outcasts of poverty,
those who ironed my clothes.

I bless the machines that washed my dirty laundry
I praise to the point of delirium
those who shoot in honor of my name,
those who killed without mercy
(following my strict orders)
a scented tiger, a lion without signs of identity.

I celebrate as expected of me, and down to a T,
those who screamed the N word at George Floyd,
those who killed Breonna Taylor
and Trayvon Martin's luminous smiles,

the blacks who run by mistake
and those who call Mexicans rapists
and those who welded the bars of the cages.

I love those who justify
this mortgage hell addicted
to the elements in open space.
I forgive my blood
my bad cholesterol
my useless health
my children
my grandchildren
I am innocent at being a grandfather.
I am guilty at being a father.
I must be incriminated for being a man.

I forgive the mummies who listened to me,
those who write my prohibitions
the bible with which I posed to fool myself.

I ridicule myself.
I'm an adorable despot.

I apologize to all my accomplices
for creating the religion of lies.

For declaring bankruptcy
to save the myth of "the superman"
for nationalizing hopelessness.

I'm sure: I was never real.
It doesn't make sense to be real off Facebook,
Twitter, WhatsApp or Messenger.
I was too unreal.
All my dreams were useless.
I don't know why I depend on the organs
that promote the banality of this poem.
Nothing on my part justifies smelling,
thinking, feeling, living, reading,
pretending, killing, existing, sitting down.

killing is good for infecting despair;
hugging or kissing others is something else.
I will sign these humiliating pardons
Like committing suicide is for cowards
It hurts me not to have forgiven Jeffrey Epstein.
I love the unwary for daring to imitate me
I adore those who lick my boots,
the fools who think they represent me,
all the immoral lackeys,
the defenders of the imbeciles,
those who hide my crimes.
My freedom was created
by a complicity with the enemies
of civilization; that's why I'm right
when I choose to forgive myself.

Tomás Modesto Galán is a Dominican writer living in New York since 1986. He is currently the founding president of the Association of Dominican Writers in the United States (ASEDEU). He is co-administrator of the page: Cultural Decolonization. Galán is also the author of *Letters from the Diaspora*, a monthly current-affairs publication. He is part of the board of directors of the Hispanic Festival of the Bronx and was the president of the Bronx Book Fair: Open Book. He has been a professor at the Autonomous University of Santo Domingo, Pace University, and the Dominican O&M University. He currently teaches at York College. He was also coordinator of the Dominican Commissioner of Culture in the United States.

Tomás Modesto Galán's essays, poems, and articles appear in magazines, on social media, and in numerous anthologies. Among his most important works, all in Spanish, are: *Los cuentos de Mount Hope* (novel, 1995) and *Los niños de Mount Eden* (stories, 1998), *Cenizas en el viento* (poetry, 1983), *Es la poesía de Juan Antonio Alix popular?* (essay, 1987), *Diario de Caverna* (poetry, 1988), *Subway* (poetry, 2008), and *Al margen del Color* (novel, 2014). In 2014, his collection of poems *Love on a Bicycle and other poems* won the

"Overseas Letters" Award. *Odisea Vital* (poetry, 2017) is his latest publication. The personal anthology *Góngora en motoconcho* (*Góngora On a Motoconcho*) collects a sample of his poetry from 1983 to 2020.

On October 16, 2015, Tomás Modesto Galán was named *Poet of the Year* by The America's Poetry Festival in New York. In 2016, he was part of the first great Poetry Reading: *Cuny Writers Against Austerity*.

Many of his texts have been translated into English, Arabic, and Portuguese. He has participated in numerous national and international festivals.

You can purchase his books at Amazon.com. For more information about his work as a cultural manager, visit his YouTube channel: Tomás Modesto Galán.

This work has been published in April 2025
in the United States of America, under the care of publisher
Books&Smith. All rights belong to the author,
and the final editing was carried out by Edgar Smith
—representing the publisher.

www.ingramcontent.com/pod-product-compliance
Lightning Source LLC
Chambersburg PA
CBHW030911120626
46554CB00001B/107